A FIRST
HISTORY OF INDIA

A FIRST HISTORY OF INDIA

H.L.O.GARRETT

GYAN

Published by

Gyan Publishing House
5, Ansari Road
Daryaganj, New Delhi-110002
Phone: 011-47034999, 9811692060
E-mail: books@gyanbooks.com

Distribution Network
gyanbooks.com
India, USA, Canada, UK, Australia

ISBN: 978-93-7097-600-9 (PB)

First Published, 1936

2nd Impression 2025

Printed at: Gyan Press, Delhi.

A FIRST HISTORY OF INDIA
Author: H.L.O.Garrett

A FIRST HISTORY OF INDIA

BY

H. L. O. GARRETT, M. A., I. E. S.
PROFESSOR OF HISTORY,
GOVERNMENT COLLEGE, LAHORE

WITH ILLUSTRATIONS AND MAPS

BOMBAY
K. & J. COOPER
EDUCATIONAL PUBLISHERS

Photo. W. and D. Downey, London.

KING GEORGE V: EMPEROR OF INDIA.

PREFACE.

Some apology is needed for the appearance of yet another History of India. In this little book the author has tried to tell the complicated story of the History of India in the simplest possible form. To this end the earlier chapters are written in a style in which an endeavour has been made to avoid difficult phrases and involved passages. They may thus be put into the hands of boys whose knowledge of English is not of an advanced nature. As the story progresses, the difficulty of the language has been deliberately increased. The author hopes that the whole may form a progressive text-book, presenting no difficulty to a student whose knowledge of English is being increased by a study of that language in other directions.

H. L. O. GARRETT

CONTENTS.

CHAP.		PAGE
I.	EARLY DAYS	1
II.	THE ARYANS	4
III.	THE BEGINNING OF INDIAN HISTORY.	9
IV.	CHANDRAGUPTA AND ASOKA	11
V.	THE NEW INVASIONS OF INDIA. KING KANISHKA	15
VI.	THE GUPTA EMPIRE	17
VII.	HARSHA OF KANAUJ, THE LAST HINDU EMPEROR	20
VIII.	THE COMING OF THE MAHOMEDANS...	23
IX.	THE EARLY MAHOMEDAN KINGDOMS...	27
X.	THE EARLY MAHOMEDAN KINGS ...	30
XI.	THE SMALLER KINGDOMS AND THE ARRIVAL OF THE PORTUGUESE ...	33
XII.	THE EARLY MOGULS: BABAR AND HUMAYUN	36
XIII.	AKBAR	39
XIV.	JEHANGIR	43
XV.	SHAH JEHAN	46
XVI.	AURUNGZEB. THE LAST OF THE GREAT MOGULS	49
XVII.	THE DECLINE AND FALL OF THE MOGUL EMPIRE	54
XVIII.	THE RISE OF THE EUROPEAN SETTLEMENTS. THE FRENCH AND ENGLISH IN THE SOUTH	61

CHAP.		PAGE
XIX.	THE ENGLISH IN BENGAL	67
XX.	CLIVE'S WORK IN BENGAL ...	72
XXI.	HAIDAR ALI, THE LION OF MYSORE	77
XXII.	WARREN HASTINGS—GOVERNOR	80
XXIII.	WARREN HASTINGS—GOVERNOR-GENERAL	84
XXIV.	WARREN HASTINGS—GOVERNOR-GENERAL. (*Continued.*)	89
XXV.	LORD CORNWALLIS	93
XXVI.	SIR JOHN SHORE	98
	MARQUESS WELLESLEY	99
XXVII.	LORD CORNWALLIS	105
	LORD MINTO	106
XXVIII.	LORD HASTINGS	111
XXIX.	LORD AMHERST	116
	LORD WILLIAM BENTINCK ...	118
XXX.	LORD AUCKLAND	122
	LORD ELLENBOROUGH	126
XXXI.	SIR HENRY HARDINGE	128
XXXII.	LORD DALHOUSIE	132
XXXIII.	LORD CANNING (THE LAST GOVERNOR-GENERAL)	138
XXXIV.	THE FIRST VICEROYS:	
	LORD CANNING	146
	LORD ELGIN	148
	SIR JOHN (LORD) LAWRENCE ...	149
XXXV.	LORD MAYO	151
	LORD NORTHBROOK	153
	LORD LYTTON	155

CHAP.		PAGE
XXXVI.	Lord Ripon	158
	Lord Dufferin	160
	Lord Lansdowne	162
	Lord Elgin	163
XXXVII.	The Later Viceroys:	
	Lord Curzon	165
	Lord Minto	167
	Lord Hardinge	169
XXXVIII.	Summary	171
	Chronological Table of Indian History	179

LIST OF ILLUSTRATIONS AND MAPS.

KING GEORGE V: EMPEROR OF INDIA. *Facing title-page.*

Facing page

ANCIENT INDIA 4
BUDDHA 8
EMPIRE OF ASOKA 13
INDIA IN KING KANISHKA'S TIME ... 16
GUPTA EMPIRE 17
EMPIRE OF HARSHA 20
KUTUB-MINAR 24
AFGHAN EMPIRE UNDER ALA-UD-DIN... 29
INDIA IN 1398 32
THE COUNCIL CHAMBER, VIJAYANAGAR 34
BABAR 36
AKBAR 40
INDIA IN 1605 41
THE TAJ MAHAL 44
SHAH JEHAN 46
MOTI MUSJID 50
AURUNGZEB 52
BOLI GUMBAZ, BIJAPUR 60
DUPLEIX 62
ROBERT CLIVE 72
WARREN HASTINGS 82
LORD CORNWALLIS 94
INDIA IN 1795 96

	Facing page
MARQUESS WELLESLEY	100
INDIA IN 1805	104
LORD HASTINGS	112
FORT OF BHARATPUR	116
INDIA IN 1823	117
LORD WILLIAM BENTINCK	120
THE KHYBER PASS	124
LORD DALHOUSIE	134
INDIA IN 1856	136
LORD CANNING	138
QUEEN VICTORIA	144
THE DELHI DURBAR OF 1903	168

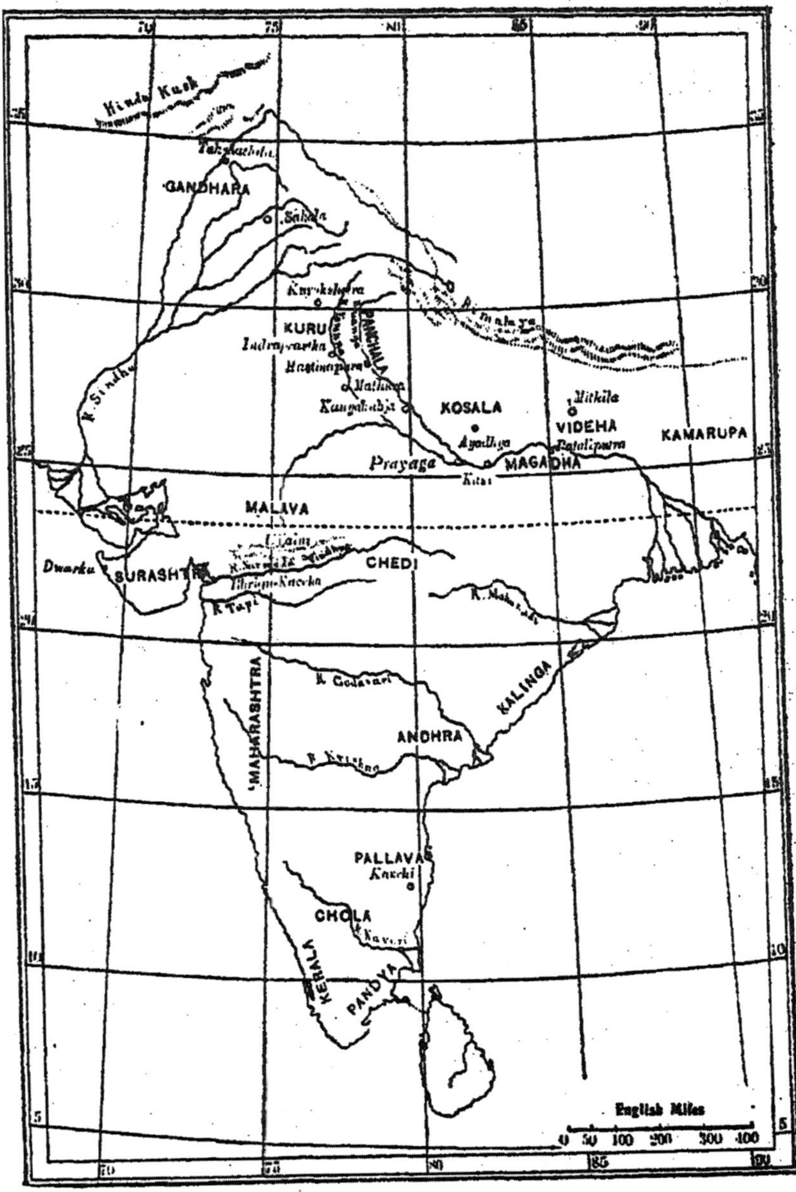

ANCIENT INDIA.

villages which they fortified to protect themselves from attacks of wild beasts and of their enemies. We also learn much of their customs, such as their marriage ceremonies and funerals.

At first each family was quite separate and independent and the father of the family was its lord or ruler. But after a time the Aryans began to be divided up into a number of small states ruled over by kings or chiefs. These kings led the people in times of war and in times of peace they acted as judges. In return for this the people of the states made offerings for their support. In earlier days these kings had also conducted the worship of the gods themselves, but now they became too busy and so a separate body of people began to grow up whose duty it was to offer sacrifices, etc. This is the beginning of the System of Castes. These men formed the Brahman caste and soon there were three other castes formed — the Rajputs or Kshattriyas whose business it was to fight, the Vaisyas who cultivated the land and engaged in business, and last of all the Sudras. The Sudras were not Aryans at all but were the descendants of the people conquered by the Aryans. They did all the lowest work and were looked upon as little better than slaves.

From the Rig Veda, and from the other sacred books which came after it, we learn much about the Brahmans. They changed the old worship of the powers of nature such as the sun, the air, etc. and began to teach the worship of the Creator of the world—Brahma. The Brahmans studied other things besides religion. They knew a good deal about medicine, and they studied the stars and planets and made a calendar of the year. They also gave laws to the people. The famous Code of Manu is a collection of these laws.

Besides the Vedas there are two other great books which tell us the stories of those early days and which are very well known to us to day. These are the Mahabharata and the Ṛamayana.

The Mahabharata is a very long poem of the kind which we call an "epic," that is, a poem which tells the story of some great deed or deeds. The principal story of the Mahabharata tells us of the fights between two royal families, the Pandavas and the Kauravas. At first the Pandavas were defeated. But after many great battles, in which many of the gods took part, the Kauravas were all slain. Finally the Pandavas were allowed to enter heaven.

The Ramayana tells us the story of Rama who was the son of a king who ruled over what is now called Oudh. In those days the country was full of monsters, called Rakshasas, who treated the people very cruelly. Rama made up his mind to rid the country of these monsters and he and his brother fought many battles against them. After this he won for his wife the princess Sita, by bending the great bow of Siva which no one else had been able to do. To keep his father's word, Rama had then to go into exile, and for some years he and Sita lived in the forest. During this time Ravana, the wicked King of Ceylon, carried off Sita. Rama found out where she was by the help of Hanuman. and then Hanuman's monkey soldiers built a bridge over to Ceylon and they all crossed over and rescued Sita. After this Rama and Sita returned to their kingdom. But the people laughed at Sita because she had been among the demons and, in the end, Rama drove her away into the forest again.

Gradually the religion taught by the Brahmans—Hinduism—spread all over Southern India and, by about 600 B.C., was the chief religion of the country. But there were people who did not like the power of the Brahmans and the way in which they had taken religion into their own hands, and soon there arose a new religious teacher who founded a new religion.

Gautama (the Buddha) was the son of the king of a small kingdom in the North of India near the Himalaya. He was born in 567 B.C. and in his earlier years lived the ordinary life of a prince. Then he left his wife and his home and retired into the woods where he became a wanderer. During these wanderings he made up his mind that the teaching of the Brahmans was wrong and that sacrifices were not necessary. On the other hand, he taught that if a man wished to be happy in a future state he must be kind to all living things and must control his own thoughts and actions. Many people followed him and he became known as the Buddha, the Enlightened One. He sent his followers all over India to preach his religion and these followers became Buddhist monks. His religion spread very widely and, though it has now almost died out in India, in other countries of the East—China, Burma, Ceylon, etc.,—many millions of people are still Buddhists.

Another religion which was started at the same time was Jainism which was founded by Mahavira. He taught that to obtain happiness in a future state a man must do years of hard penance. Like Buddha he taught his followers to be kind to all living things and not to take the life of anything.

Photo. Johnston and Hoffman, Calcutta.

BUDDHA.

CHAPTER III.

THE BEGINNING OF INDIAN HISTORY.

Persian invasion of India — Alexander's invasion of India.

A great deal of what we have learnt of the early days in India is only guess work, because at that time there were no regular books and stories were simply handed on from one man to another. But about 550 B. C. — about the time that Buddha was beginning to preach his new religion — we do begin to know more about India, more especially about the North, for we do not know much about Southern India till much later. At that time the North of India was divided into a number of little kingdoms. The most important of these was a kingdom called Magadha which was the kingdom where Buddha began his preaching. It lay in the North East near the Himalaya and a number of strong kings extended its power over the kingdoms lying near it. During this time (from about 550 -- 320 B. C.) the two most important events were the two invasions of India by armies from outside. First of all, about 500 B. C., the Persians, in the reign of their great king Darius, sent armies to the western part of the Punjab and conquered it, and for some years it was a province of the Persian Empire.

The second and more important invasion was that of Alexander the Great. Alexander was first of all king of Macedonia, a small state to the north of Greece; but he was a great soldier and with a well trained army he conquered Greece and afterwards invaded Asia and overthrew the Persian power. In 327 B. C. he invaded India, crossed the Indus and won a great battle on the Jhelum. He then went on conquering the North of India and in three years conquered the whole of the Punjab and Sind. He intended to conquer the whole of India but his soldiers refused to go on any further. So he was obliged to stop at the river Beas. He probably meant to come back but he died (323 B. C.) before he could do so. Many traces are left of Alexander's invasion. Coins have been found and some ruins of buildings show the Greek style which Alexander brought into the country. We know a good deal about Alexander's invasion because many of the Greeks in his army wrote accounts of their journey which we still have to-day. Alexander is considered one of the greatest generals in the history of the world and it is wonderful that he did so much, considering that his own kingdom was such a small one. His success was due to the way in which his army was organized. He arranged his infantry in a solid mass, called a phalanx, which it was very difficult to break.

CHAPTER IV.

CHANDRAGUPTA AND ASOKA.

Chandragupta Maurya — Megasthenes' account — Asoka — His Edicts — Asoka and Buddhism — The Decline of the Maurya Empire — The Andhra kingdom.

Alexander had left some troops in India but upon his death these were driven out by Chandragupta, a prince of the Magadha kingdom. Before long he had conquered the whole of the North of India and he then went further and fought with Seleucus, one of Alexander's generals, who had set up a kingdom to the north of what is now Afghanistan. Seleucus was one of many of Alexander's generals, who divided up the great empire of their master upon his death. He invaded India but was beaten by Chandragupta who forced him to give up the greater part of what is now Afghanistan. Chandragupta's kingdom — which is called the Maurya Empire — was thus of very large size and his successors made it even larger. A Greek ambassador, named Megasthenes, visited his court at Pataliputra (Patna) and has given us a description of the riches and magnificence of the king. He tells us of the splendid court of the king with its gold vessels, and of the elephants with golden cloth upon them and hangings of pearls. He also tells us of the amusements of the court: how races were held between chariots drawn by oxen and how the king went out hunting.

From the same writer we learn something of the way in which the country was governed. He tells us that the king had six boards or committees to help and advise him and that the different provinces were ruled by viceroys or governors much as they are to-day.

We know very little of the next king, Bindusara, who came to the throne about 299 B. C. but his son Asoka, who became king in about 272 B. C., is much more famous. He extended his empire so that it covered nearly all India. To the North, part of Afghanistan, Kashmir and Baluchistan belonged to it, while in the South it reached as far as Madras.

Asoka was a great ruler and was a great follower of the teachings of Buddha. In order that his people might know these teachings he caused a number of "edicts"—as they were called—to be carved upon pillars, wells, etc., and many of these have come down to us. These edicts taught the people the chief principles of Buddha—to be truthful and upright--to be respectful to authority and to be kindly and courteous to one's fellow men—and to avoid taking life. Asoka showed himself a good friend to the poor and needy and set an example to every one by his kindly deeds. He punished severely any of his

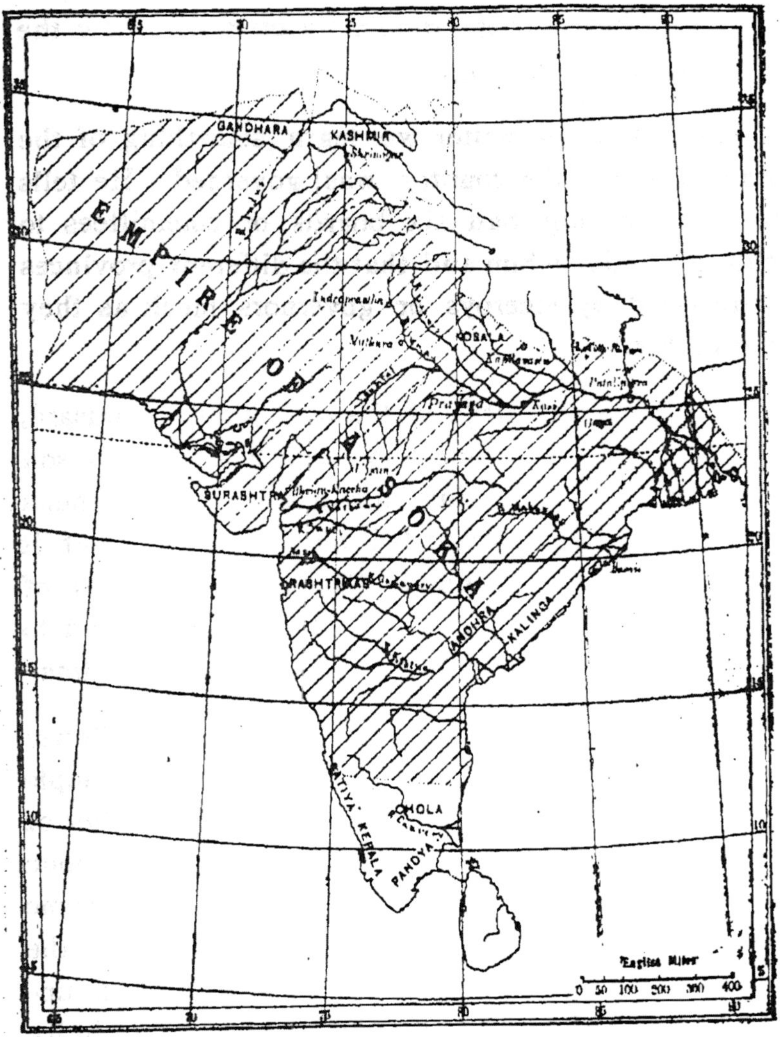

EMPIRE OF ASOKA.

officers who were guilty of cruelty. In his reign much was done for the comfort of travellers. Trees were planted to give them shade and wells were dug to provide them with water. This great king was also a great protector of animals. Cruelty to them was forbidden and all over his kingdom sick animals were well treated and looked after. Although Asoka himself was a follower of Buddha he did not interfere with the other religions of India. All good men, of whatever religion they were, were respected by the king.

Asoka was so earnest a follower of Buddha that he was anxious that other countries also should learn of the teaching of Buddha. For this purpose he sent Buddhist monks to preach their religion in Ceylon and Tibet and even in Africa and Europe. In his own country many Buddhist shrines and monasteries are said to have been built by him. Towards the end of his reign he himself became a Buddhist monk. He died about 232 B. C. and was one of the greatest kings who ever ruled in India. Like the great Akbar and like our King Emperor of to-day he was always thinking and working for the good of the people over whom he ruled.

Asoka's empire did not keep its power long after his death. His descendants, of whom we know very little, grew weaker and weaker till they were driven off the throne. Two dynasties followed them — the Sunga and the Kanva — but the kingdom of Magadha had ceased to be powerful. The most powerful kingdom in India during this period was the Andhra kingdom. This kingdom had been part of Asoka's empire but soon after his death it became independent. The Andhra kings were Dravidians — that is, they belonged to the original inhabitants of India. They gradually extended their power until they ruled over the whole of Central India and part of the North. But their power in that direction was checked by new invaders of India.

CHAPTER V.

THE NEW INVASIONS OF INDIA.

KING KANISHKA.

The Sakas—The Pallavas—Kanishka—Kanishka and Buddhism.

About 160 B. C. new invaders began to appear in India from the North. They were warlike tribes from Central Asia. If we study the history of Europe we shall find that Europe too was invaded by people from the same place, and that finally they broke into Europe and became the ancestors of the modern nations there. It was the same in India. The first of the new invaders were called the Sakas. They invaded the north-western part of India—Sind and part of the Punjab—and, though they were at one time conquered by the Andhra kings, they became independent again. About the same time some other invaders, who were called the Pallavas, also came into India from the North. However, as they could not make a home for themselves in Northern India, they made their way to the South where they set up a kingdom of their own.

The next invaders from the North were another tribe from Central Asia. They gradually conquered the country to the North of India, where there was still a kingdom ruled over by a great family of kings, descendants of one of Alexander's generals. They then conquered Kashmir and the greater part of Afghanistan and as they grew stronger they made their way further into the North of India. These invaders belonged to the Kushan tribe and the most important of them was King Kanishka who became king about 120 A. D. and ruled to 150 A. D.

Kanishka was a great king and ruled over a very large kingdom. He conquered Kashmir and so much of the territory to the North of India that he ruled over more land outside India than inside it. In the South his kingdom reached down to the river Jumna. His capital was Purushapura (Peshawar). Kanishka was a great supporter of the Buddhist religion.

By this time a great many changes had come into Buddhism and, in order to settle a great many disputed points, King Kanishka called a Great Council in Kashmir of all the leading Buddhists. The result of this Council was that the Buddhists became divided into two parties—those who followed the older forms of the religion and those who followed the newer forms.

The Kushan Empire lost most of its power after the death of Kanishka and soon ceased to be of any importance.

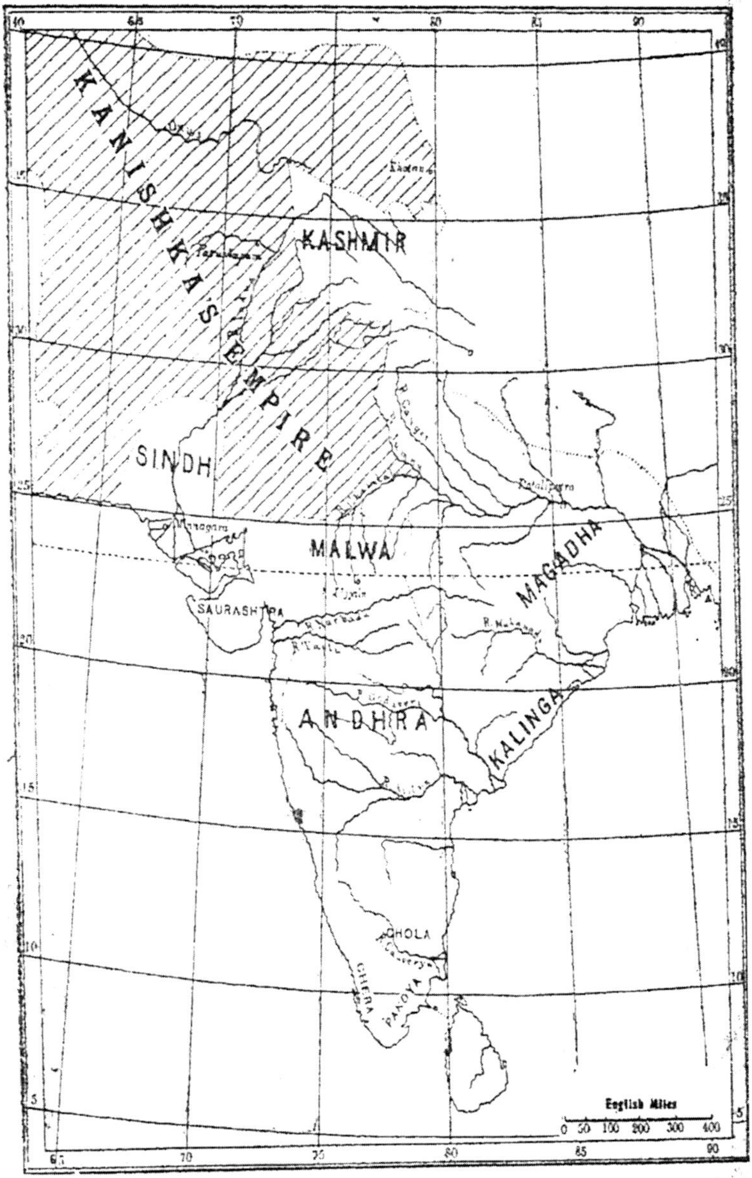

INDIA IN KING KANISHKA'S TIME.

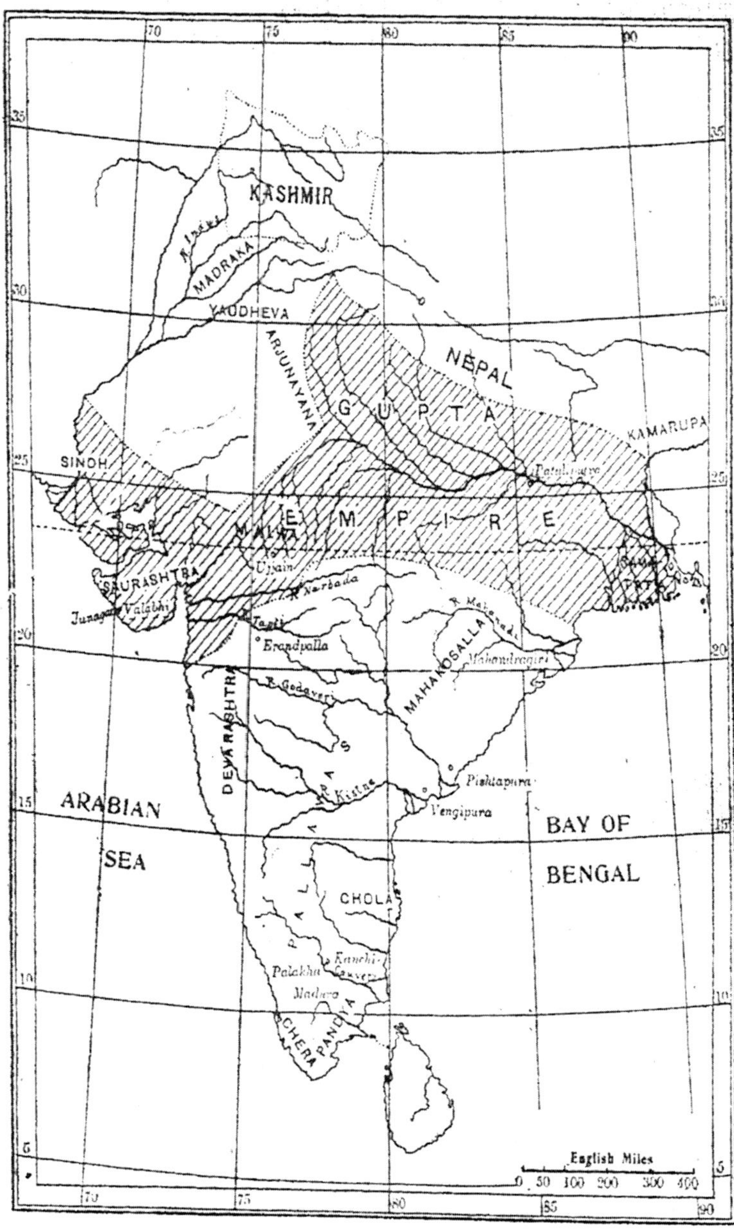

GUPTA EMPIRE.

CHAPTER VI.

THE GUPTA EMPIRE.

Chandragupta — Samudragupta — Chandragupta Vikramaditya — Fa-hien's account of India — Revival of Hinduism — Kalidas and the golden age of Sanskrit Literature.

The next empire of any importance was the Gupta Empire. This began with Chandragupta, a small chief in the neighbourhood of Patna. He gradually conquered the surrounding country until in 320 A. D. he became ruler of quite a large empire in the Eastern part of India. Upon his death he was succeeded by his son Samudragupta (326-375 A. D.) who proved himself a very great king. He was a good soldier and a clever ruler, and we are able to learn a good deal about him because he caused the story of his deeds to be carved upon a stone pillar which is still in existence and also because many relics of his time have come down to us. Samudragupta fought many wars against the neighbouring kingdoms and before his death his empire reached as far as the Nerbudda to the South. In religion he was a Hindu, but he was tolerant of other religions and he protected the Buddhists. Many pilgrims of this religion were now beginning to come to India from China, Burma, and the other

Buddhist countries in order to visit the sacred places connected with Buddha. Samudragupta's successor was his son Chandragupta Vikramaditya (375-413 A.D.) who still further extended the Gupta Empire. He conquered the Saka kingdom in the west—which had been independent since the days of the Andhra Empire—and made himself ruler of Malwa. During his reign many more Buddhist pilgrims visited the country and one of them, a Chinese monk called Fa-hien, wrote a book about his travels from which we can learn a great deal about the life in India in those days.

Travelling in those days was a difficult and dangerous matter, but Fa-hien was a very religious man and was very anxious to visit the country where Buddha had been born. When he arrived in India he found the people pleased to see him and ready to treat him kindly. He stayed nearly eleven years in India, so that he knew a good deal about the country. In his book he tells us that the people were happy and contented and that the laws under which they were governed were not harsh and cruel as they had been under some of the earlier kings. The towns were large and prosperous. Good order was kept everywhere and travellers were not attacked by robbers upon the roads. The poor were well treated by the government who gave money for their support. After the death of Chandragupta Vikramaditya two more kings ruled over the Gupta

Empire and then it came to an end, about 480 A. D. During the reign of the last king, Skandagupta, the country was much troubled by invaders from the North.

In the time of the Guptas Hinduism grew very largely and Buddhism began to be less popular. But there was no quarrel between the followers of the two religions and a good many customs of one religion began to be copied by the other. At this time also the Sanskrit language reached its highest level. Many great writers lived during this period and their writings have come down to us to-day. One of them was the famous poet Kalidasa whose poems are still read by people who can read Sanskrit.

CHAPTER VII.

HARSHA OF KANAUJ, THE LAST HINDU EMPEROR.

Invasion of the Huns—Harsha of Kanauj—Hiuen-tsang's account of Harsha's kingdom—Pulikesin II. of the Chalukya dynasty—The rise of the Rajputs—Rajaraja Deva..

The fall of the Gupta Empire was caused by the invasions of a fierce people from Central Asia called the Huns. During the early part of the sixth century they conquered and ruled over the North of India, but they behaved so cruelly that the different Indian kingdoms rose against them and drove them out. After the Huns were driven out India remained for some years divided into a number of small states, and then at the beginning of the seventh century a new power arose in Northern India. This was the kingdom of Harsha. King Harsha ruled over a kingdom which reached from the Bay of Bengal to the Sutlej and many of the neighbouring kingdoms were his vassals. We learn a good deal of this reign from the Chinese pilgrims who visited the country. One of them, a learned monk called Hiuen-tsang, stayed a number of years and wrote an account of what he saw. King Harsha was a strong ruler and governed his kingdom firmly. He was a Buddhist

EMPIRE OF HARSHA.

by religion but protected the other religions of India. King Harsha was a great scholar himself and a great patron of learned men. His capital was at Kanauj and wise men came to his court from all parts of India. His empire lasted about forty years and after his death in 648 A. D. it soon broke up.

While Harsha's empire was the strongest state in Northern India, another great state ruled in the South. This was the kingdom, called the Deccan kingdom, ruled over by a dynasty called the Chalukya. The most famous king of this dynasty was king Pulikesin II. (608-42). He was a great warrior and a great ruler, and all the neighbouring countries in the South of India were obedient to him. His fame was so great that even the king of Persia sent an ambassador to him. The Chinese pilgrim Hiuen-tsang visited this kingdom also and tells us of its greatness in his books.

There was war between King Harsha and King Pulikesin, and the former sent an army to invade the Deccan but it was defeated and driven away. The Chalukya kings belonged to a new people who rose to a very powerful position in India. These were the Rajputs. It is not quite certain where they originally came from, but they were a famous race, very fond of fighting and very brave in battle. In religion they were Hindus and, during the time of their rule in India, the Hindu religion gradually took the place of the Buddhist and the latter died out. As a result of this there are hardly any Buddhists in India to-day. The Hindu religion itself was changed and instead of the old form which was called the Vedic a new form called the Puranic was introduced.

In the North of India also, as in the South, the Rajputs became the leading people. We have seen how after the death of King Harsha his empire broke up. In its place there were formed a number of small states and in these states the Rajputs speedily got the upper hand. They were a nation of warriors and were divided into a number of clans or tribes, which made it easy to collect an army for fighting. Then by the beginning of the eleventh century nearly all India was under the Rajputs. In Bengal, however, there were a number of small states which were not under them and in the extreme South there were three ancient kingdoms ruled over by kings of Dravidian family. One of these, the Chola kingdom, became famous under a king called Rajaraja Deva, and during his reign, about 1000 A. D., the Chola kingdom was large and powerful.

CHAPTER VIII.

THE COMING OF THE MAHOMEDANS.

Mahomed, the Prophet of Islam—Mahomed bin Kasim—Mahomed of Ghazni—Mahomed Ghori—Jai Chand and Prithvi Raj—First and second battles of Tarain.

In the sixth century a new religion was founded which had a great effect upon the history of the world and particularly upon India. Mahomed, who was born in 570 A. D. at Mecca in Arabia, became the founder of a religion of which he was the prophet. At first the people of Arabia did not listen to his teaching, but gradually the number of his followers increased until all Arabia acknowledged him. Mahomed died in 632 and after his death his successors, who were called the Caliphs, led large armies to conquer the neighbouring countries and to spread their new religion, which was called Islam. The Caliphs conquered all the North of Africa and then crossed over to Europe and occupied Spain. In the East they conquered Persia and set up an Empire with its capital at Bagdad. They were a learned and clever people and Bagdad became a great centre of civilization. Before long they began to extend their conquests further, and in 712 the first Mahomedan army arrived in India. It was led by a general called Mahomed bin Kasim and it came into

India by way of the Persian Gulf. After winning a great battle the Mahomedans conquered the whole of Sind and settled down there. But the province soon ceased to be a part of the Bagdad Empire and so the first invasion did not have much effect upon India.

The next invasion was more serious. The Caliphs had conquered a huge empire but they could not keep it. In the middle of the tenth century their power was overthrown by an invasion of a fierce people called the Turks, who came from Central Asia. These Turks adopted the Mahomedan religion and, being a very warlike people, began to extend their conquests. They seized the whole of Afghanistan and one of their leaders set up his capital at Ghazni, and it was his son, the famous Mahomed of Ghazni, who was to be the first real Mahomedan conqueror in India.

Mahomed's first invasion of India took place in 1000 A. D. He fought and won a great battle against Jaipal, the Rajput ruler of Lahore. Although the Rajputs fought very bravely they were utterly defeated and Jaipal was taken prisoner. He was afterwards set free but, unable to bear the disgrace, he burned himself upon a pyre. His son Anangpal also fought against Mahomed and he also was defeated. Altogether Mahomed invaded India sixteen times. In 1018 he destroyed the famous city of Kanauj which had been the capital of King Harsha, and in 1026 he captured

Photo. Johnston and Hoffman, Calcutta.

KUTUB-MINAR.

the famous sacred city of Somnath and took away with him to Ghazni the great gates of the temple. During these years of fighting he conquered the whole of the Punjab. But he did not really care for increasing his empire. He was a very pious Mahomedan and he fought all these wars in order to add glory to his religion. In India men called him the "Idol-breaker" because he destroyed the Hindu temples and images and carried off the treasure from them. Although he was so fierce an enemy of the Hindus, in his own capital of Ghazni he was a great supporter of learning. He founded a university and gathered at his court a number of poets, philosophers and learned men.

Mahomed died in 1030 and on his death his sons began quarrelling over his empire. As a result of this they became weak and were attacked and defeated by the rulers of Ghor, another small state in Afghanistan. In 1174 a prince of this family, the famous Mahomed Ghori, became the ruler. This great soldier invaded India many times.

At this time the principal Hindu rulers in the North of India were the Rajput kings Jai Chand of Kanauj and Prithvi Raj Chauhan of Ajmer and Delhi. But these rulers were not on good terms. Jai Chand had tried to conquer all the lands of the Rajputs and Prithvi Raj had resisted him and had carried off his daughter by force and married her. This caused great enmity between them and when Jai Chand also heard that Prithvi Raj had found a treasure at Chitor, which had remained there for many years, he was afraid that Prithvi Raj would become too powerful.

For this reason he and some of the other Rajput rulers called in the help of Mahomed Ghori. Mahomed came with a great army and met Prithvi Raj on the battlefield of Tarain, about fourteen miles from Thaneswar, in 1191. Although the soldiers of Mahomed fought very bravely they could not resist the Rajputs and were defeated with great slaughter. Mahomed Ghori himself was wounded in the battle. In the next year, however, he came back again and again fought the Rajputs under Prithvi Raj on the same battlefield of Tarain. This time he was victorious and Prithvi Raj was captured. A year later, he attacked Kanauj, drove out Jai Chand and took possession of his kingdom. Mahomed then went back to his own country and left one of his generals Kutb-ud-din Aybek — who had originally been one of his slaves — as his Viceroy in India. Kutb-ud-din and other generals went on with the conquest of India. Gwalior, Behar and Bengal were all conquered. In the end Mahomed's empire — which is called the Afghan Empire — reached over the whole of the North of India. Mahomed died in 1206 and on his death his Viceroy Kutb-ud-din set himself up as king at Delhi, and from this time onwards there was always a Mahomedan king at Delhi until 1857.

CHAPTER IX.

THE EARLY MAHOMEDAN KINGDOMS.

Kutb-ud-din, the first of the Slave Kings—Altamsh—Rezia—Balban—The Khilji Kings—Ala-ud-din—Malik Kafur's conquest of the South—Kutb-ud-din Mubarak.

We have seen how, when Mahomed died in 1206, his Viceroy Kutb-ud-din made himself king of Delhi. Kutb-ud-din had been originally a slave and for that reason he and his successors are known as the Slave Kings. We can still see at Delhi the famous monument called the Kutub-Minar which was built by these early Slave kings. Kutb-ud-din died in 1210 and was succeeded by another slave, Altamsh, in whose reign the first large coins were made from which our modern rupee is derived. Altamsh, who died in 1236, was succeeded by his son who died very soon and then by his daughter, Rezia. The latter was a brave woman and tried to rule like a man and to lead armies, but a rebellion took place and she was deposed. Her brother, who succeeded her, was weak and the power passed into the hands of one of his generals, Balban. Balban, who also had been a slave, was a brave and skilful general and drove away the Mongols who tried to invade India during this period. When the king died Balban became ruler in his place and ruled over the North of India from 1266 to 1287. He proved an able king and kept good order in his dominions. Rebellions were put down with great sternness and the armies were carefully drilled and kept ready for action, in case any more invasion should take place.

Upon Balban's death another dynasty of kings came to throne. They were descended from an Afghan tribe, called the Khilji, which had come into India at the time of the Turkish invasion. The first of these kings was a weak man and was killed by his nephew Ala-ud-din who became king in 1296. He was a warrior king, fierce and cruel. No sooner did he become king than he found himself attacked by invaders from the North. These were the Mongols or Tartars. Ala-ud-din marched against these invaders in 1297 and utterly defeated them near Delhi. After their defeat many of them became Mahomedans and remained in India. But afterwards Ala-ud-din became suspicious of them and had them all murdered.

Ala-ud-din then attacked the Rajput state of Chitor. He had heard that the wife of the Raja was the most beautiful woman in India and he wanted to carry her off. At first he was unsuccessful, for the fortress of Chitor was a very strong one and he could not take it. But he came back again in 1303 and surrounded the fortress very closely. At last the Rajputs saw that they could not hold out any longer. But the wife of the Raja and other Rajput ladies

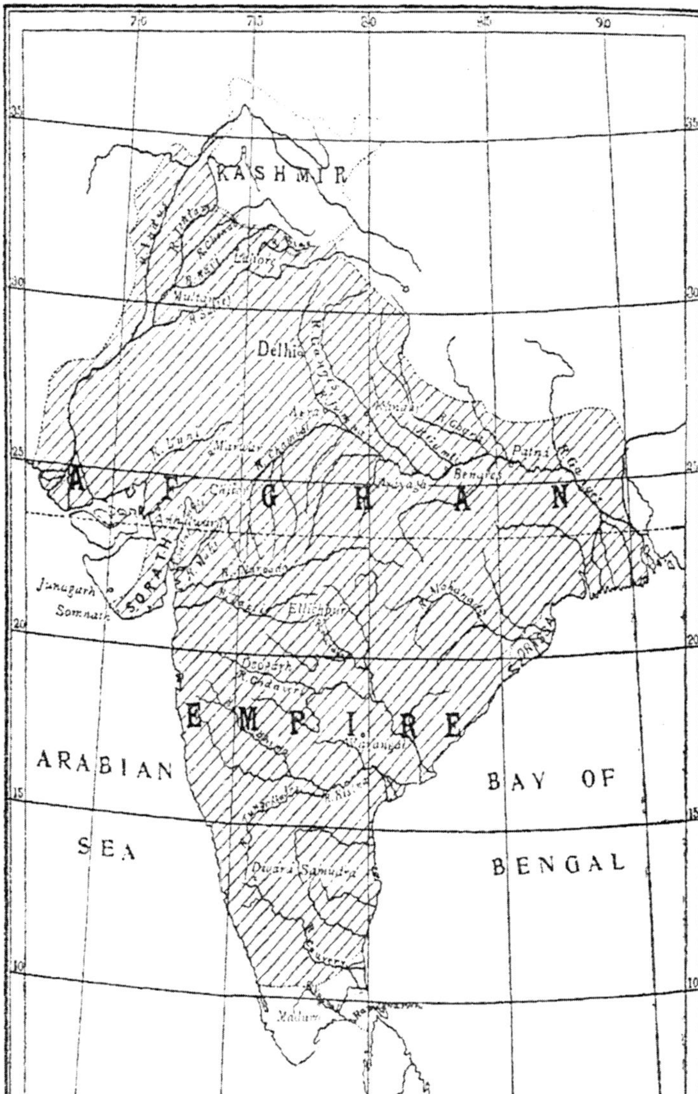

AFGHAN EMPIRE UNDER ALA-UD-DIN.

made up their minds that they would not be taken prisoners by Ala-ud-din. So they lighted a great funeral pyre in the fortress and all of them threw themselves upon it. Then the Raja and his brave followers opened the gates of the fortress and went on fighting bravely till they were all killed.

After this Ala-ud-din sent armies to invade the Deccan. His general, Malik Kafur, fought three great campaigns there and conquered the whole of the Deccan and defeated the Hindu rulers of the extreme South. These conquests brought great wealth to Ala-ud-din and he called himself the "Second Alexander." As a ruler he was very cruel. He was always afraid that his nobles might plot against him so that he treated them with great severity. The common people were very heavily taxed, especially the Hindus, and the tax collectors were very brutal in gathering the taxes.

The result was that, when he died in 1316, all was confusion till a new king Kutb-ud-din Mubarak came to the throne. The new king was cruel and lived a very evil life. His reign was only a short one, for he was murdered by one of his favourites who seized the throne and proved an even worse ruler. At last he was killed by a leader called Ghias-ud-din Tughlak who became the first of a new line of kings, called the Tughlak dynasty.

CHAPTER X.

THE EARLY MAHOMEDAN KINGS. (*Continued.*)

Ghias-ud-din Tughlak—Mahomed Tughlak—Firoz Shah Tughlak—Tamerlane's invasion of India—Break-up of the old Delhi Empire.

Ghias-ud-din Tughlak reigned for a very short time but during his reign he proved a wise and merciful ruler. Bengal was reconquered and added to his empire. His son Mahomed Tughlak (1325-1351) was a man of very savage temper and tried to rule his empire by fear. Dreadful punishments were inflicted upon those who rebelled against him. His reign is chiefly remembered because he tried to move his capital from Delhi to a new town 700 miles away, which he called Daulatabad. But the whole plan was a failure and a great many of the people, whom he had ordered to remove to the new city, died, and he was obliged to go back to Delhi. The cruelty of the king ruined his empire and many provinces revolted and broke away. When he died he was succeeded by his cousin Firoz Shah (1351-1388). Firoz Shah was a wise and kindly ruler. He restored order and put down rebellion. During his reign the people were contented and well governed.

Firoz Shah had a very wise minister as his adviser whose name was Makbul Khan. By his advice he forgave the people their debts and so the country became more prosperous. In order to increase the prosperity of the country he also made a number of canals from the Jumna to the Sutlej and in other parts of his kingdom. We know to-day how important canals are in India and how the Government is always opening new ones.

Firoz Shah was fond of magnificence and show and during his reign many new cities were built. Upon his death in 1388 a period of dreadful confusion followed. There was no one strong enough to put down disorder and the empire broke up into a number of small states. It was at this time that India was again invaded from the North. In 1398 the famous Timur or Tamerlane appeared in India. Like many of the invaders of India he came from Central Asia, and he was the leader of a people called the Mongols or Moghuls as they were afterwards called. Timur was a Mahomedan and, like many of the Mahomedan invaders, he did not wish to remain in India but only to gain glory for his religion by making war upon the Hindus. He marched through the Punjab, killing and burning as he went, and then arrived at Delhi where a great battle was fought. In the battle the king of Delhi was defeated, and Timur then entered Delhi and plundered it. After staying there only a few days Timur marched north again, plundering and burning, and went back to his own kingdom in Central Asia, leaving everything in confusion behind him. After Timur's invasion the old empire of Delhi broke up altogether. It had been getting weaker and weaker for some time and now it disappeared and India was divided again into a number of small kingdoms.

INDIA IN 1398.

CHAPTER XI.

THE SMALLER KINGDOMS AND THE ARRIVAL OF THE PORTUGUESE.

The kingdom of Vijayanagar—The Bahmani kingdom—The kingdoms of Malwa and Gujerat—The kingdoms of Bengal and Jaunpur—The Portuguese in India—Vasco da Gama—Albuquerque.

We have seen how the old Delhi empire broke up, after the invasion of Timur, into a number of small kingdoms. This only made India weaker and, as we shall see, when the next invasion came, made it much more easy for the whole country to be conquered. Let us now see into what small kingdoms India became divided.

Starting from the south we find first of all the kingdom of Vijayanagar. This was a Hindu kingdom and took up the whole of the extreme South of India. To the north of this there was founded a kingdom in the Deccan called the Bahmani kingdom—a Mahomedan kingdom which was constantly at war with Vijayanagar. The Bahmani kingdom was at one time very powerful but by the beginning of the sixteenth century it had split up into a number of smaller kingdoms. North of this came the kingdoms of Malwa and Gujerat.

These kingdoms were also constantly at war with one another and finally Malwa was conquered by Gujerat. North of these again came Sind and Rajputana. In the East were two other kingdoms, Bengal and Jaunpur. Bengal was a powerful kingdom which had been independent for a number of years. Jaunpur, which included Oudh and Behar, was at one time a powerful kingdom but it was reconquered by the old Delhi empire just at the end of the fifteenth century. The old empire of Delhi was reduced to a part of the Punjab and was ruled over by a family called the Lodi kings.

During this period we first hear of the arrival of European ships in India. In 1498 the famous Portuguese sailor Vasco da Gama finished his great voyage round Africa and across the Indian Ocean and arrived at Calicut. Ever since Constantinople had been taken by the Turks in 1453, and the road to India by land closed, the Portuguese, who were the best sailors in Europe, had been trying to get to India by sea. When they did arrive in India they built a factory at Calicut and started trading. But as they also tried to convert the people to Christianity they quarrelled with the local rulers. They were also attacked by the Arabs, who did most of the business in the Indian Ocean and did not want anyone else to come there. However the Portuguese sent out a great leader called Albuquerque in 1507, who defeated the Arabs and planted a

Photo. Johnston and Hoffman, Calcutta.

THE COUNCIL CHAMBER, VIJAYANAGAR.

Portuguese settlement at Goa. This he fortified so that it was too strong to be attacked and from this place he did business with the country round. Goa became the centre of a great trade and Portuguese ships traded from that port to more distant parts of the East Indies.

CHAPTER XII.

THE EARLY MOGULS : BABAR AND HUMAYUN.

Babar—First battle of Panipat—Battle of Kanwaha—Character of Babar—Humayun—Exile of Humayun—Sher Shah—Return of Humayun.

We have seen how, early in the sixteenth century, the old empire of Delhi had been reduced to a very small kingdom round Delhi itself. This kingdom was ruled over by a family of kings called the Lodi kings. In 1518, when one of these kings died, a number of his relations claimed the throne and one of them fled to Kabul to ask help from the ruler there. This ruler was the famous Babar. He ruled over a small Mogul kingdom and all his life he had been engaged in fighting so that he was a skilful soldier. Although he was no longer young, he at once decided to invade India and in 1525 he marched into the Punjab. The king of Delhi marched out to meet him and a great battle was fought at Panipat not far from Delhi. In this battle the king of Delhi was killed and Babar and his army then entered Delhi. Babar now became king but there was still much to be done before the country was really conquered. The Rajputs, the bravest of the Hindus, rose against the new invader. Babar, and

Photo. Bourne and Shepherd, India.

BABAR.

his son Humayun, marched against them and defeated them in the great battle of Kanwaha (1527). After this Babar defeated the remains of the armies of the Lodi kings and forced them to make peace.

In 1530 Babar died, after a very short reign, during which he had done a very great deal. He died at Agra which he had made his capital and where he had built himself a palace. We shall see that, like Babar, nearly all the great Mogul rulers are famous for the beautiful palaces and buildings which they erected and for the beautiful gardens which they laid out.

Babar, although he was a great conqueror, was not simply a rough soldier. In victory he showed himself kind and merciful to the defeated. He was a well educated man and was fond of music and poetry. He wrote an account of his life which has come down to us and which tells us a good deal about this great king.

Before he died he began to settle his kingdom and to divide it into districts so that the taxes could be collected properly and paid into his treasury.

Upon the death of Babar his son Humayun became king. Humayun was a brave and clever ruler but he was not so strong a man as his father had been. In the first part of his reign he met with a great many misfortunes. First of all his brother, the king of Kabul, took the Punjab away from him and then

Bahadur Shah, the king of Gujerat, prepared to invade his kingdom. Humayun marched against Bahadur Shah and defeated him, but no sooner had he done so than a rebellion broke out against him in Bengal, under a leader called Sher Khan. Humayun made the mistake of not attacking him at once before he grew too strong. When he did march against him, Sher Khan, by means of a trick, made a sudden attack upon him and destroyed nearly all his army (1539). Humayun managed to escape, and in the next year met Sher Khan once more in the battle of Kanauj (1540). Here he was completely defeated, and for fifteen years was driven out of his kingdom. During that time he managed to defeat his brother, the king of Kabul, and take his kingdom from him.

In the meantime Sher Khan had seized Delhi and made himself king under the name of Sher Shah. During his short reign of five years he proved himself an able and just ruler and treated all his subjects, Hindus and Mahomedans alike, with equal fairness. He was killed in battle in 1545 and his successors were not strong enough to keep down rebellion. Great disorder broke out and in the middle of this, Humayun, who had managed to win the kingdom of Kabul, marched down into India to get back his kingdom. He won a great battle in the Punjab and in 1555 he once more occupied Delhi. But before he could reconquer the whole of his kingdom he died, as the result of a fall, in 1556 and was succeeded by his son, the great Akbar.

CHAPTER XIII.

AKBAR (1556-1605).

Akbar—Second battle of Panipat—Akbar's conquests—His wise policy—His administration—His treatment of the Hindus—The Urdu language—Abul Fazl.

Before his death Humayun had not succeeded in getting back the whole of his kingdom, so that as soon as Akbar became emperor he found enemies on all sides. His first duty was to drive away these enemies. Akbar was only a boy at the time but he was very much helped by his tutor, a wise and clever man called Bairam Khan. By his advice Akbar marched against his enemies and won the great battle of Panipat (1556). This great victory gave him the whole of the North West of India. It was the beginning of a number of victories and conquests which made Akbar the ruler of a very large empire. From Afghanistan and Kashmir in the north to the river Godaveri in the south all the country became subject to him. To the south of that river lay the kingdoms of Bijapur and Golconda which Akbar never conquered. Akbar was the real founder of the Mogul Empire, and he organized his empire so well that it lasted for many years after his death. He was one of the greatest emperors who ever ruled in India. We must now consider in what way he conquered and governed his large empire.

First of all in his conquests Akbar always showed himself very merciful to the conquered. He very often took the rulers of the conquered countries into his own service, and even when they sometimes rebelled against him he did not put them to death as other kings would have done. Then he treated the people of the conquered countries kindly and did not force them to pay heavy taxes. The result was that they soon grew happy under his rule.

In order to govern his empire better Akbar divided it into fifteen provinces called Subahs. Over each province was a governor who ruled the province and arranged for the collection of taxes. The taxes were bigger than those of to-day, but the government helped the people in times of distress by allowing them to borrow money from it on easy terms. The officials were ordered not to treat the people harshly and the people had the right to complain if they did so.

In order to have a strong army always ready for war, Akbar divided the country into a number of districts, each under an officer who was bound to supply a certain number of soldiers in time of war. This reminds us of the way in which armies were collected in Europe in the Middle Ages.

Photo. Bourne and Shepherd, India.

AKBAR.

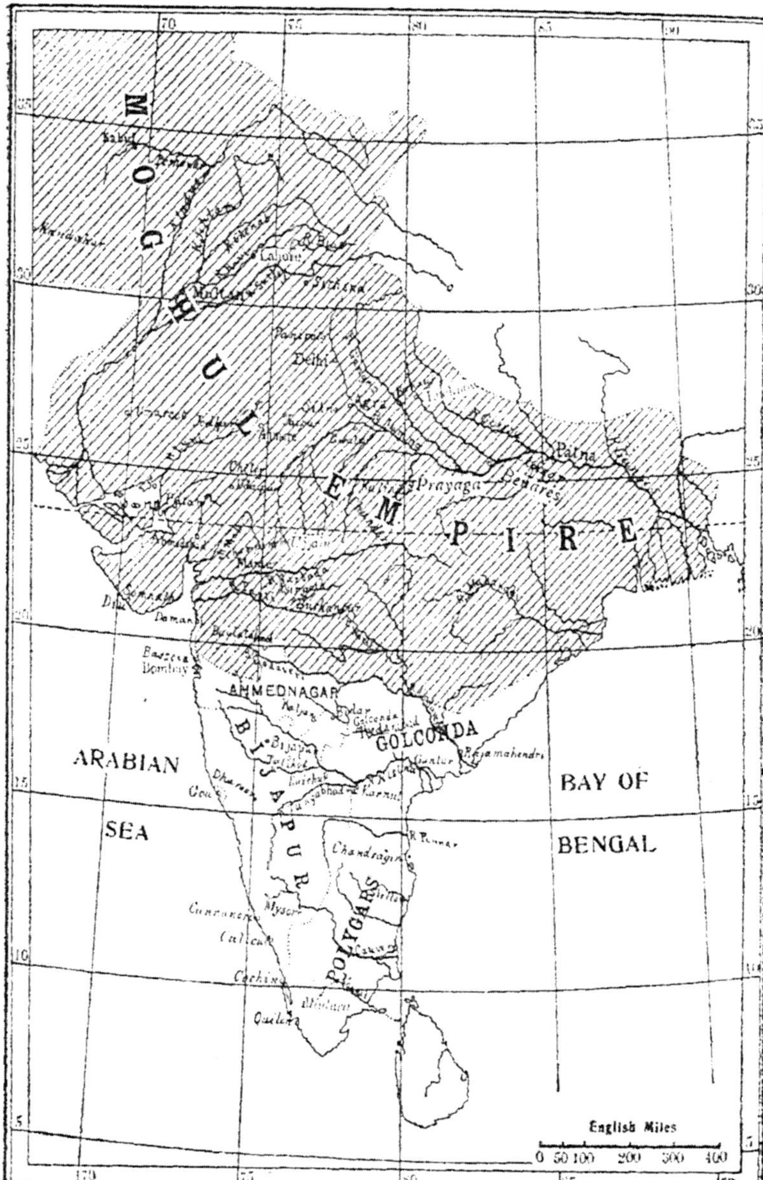

INDIA IN 1605.

Akbar treated Hindus and Mahomedans alike. He employed both in his service and some of his greatest friends and advisers were Hindus. One of the greatest was the Rajah Todar Mal. Another was the Rajput Rajah of Jaipur whose sister Akbar married. Akbar fought against some of the Rajputs and captured the great fortress of Chitor in 1567. After this the Rajputs submitted to him and Akbar married another Rajput princess, the daughter of the Rajah of Bikanir. The Rajputs were brave men, but they were not ashamed to submit to one who was so great and so wise a leader. Akbar further made the Hindus contented with his rules by doing away with the Jaziya—the tax which the other Mahomedan kings had forced the Hindus to pay.

Some of the Hindu customs Akbar did not approve of, such as Sati, and these he forbade.

During his reign the Urdu language began to be formed. The language of his court was Persian, and, as the Hindus who were in his service had to learn Persian, a mixed language began to be used out of which was formed the Urdu language which is spoken to-day.

One of Akbar's great friends was the writer Abul Fazl who wrote a history of the reign of his master, called the Ain-i-Akbari, which tells us a great deal about the government of this great king. In the last years of his reign his son prince Salim rebelled against him and had Abul Fazl murdered. This was a great grief to the old king and he soon afterwards died in 1605.

Akbar was one of the greatest of kings and his reign is a pattern of wise and good government.

CHAPTER XIV.

JEHANGIR (1605-1627).

Jehangir — Nur Jehan — English visitors to the Court of Jehangir.

Prince Salim on becoming Emperor took the title of Jehangir (Conqueror of the World). He was not so great a man as his father and he spoilt his life by heavy drinking, though he was wise enough not to let this interfere with his work during the day. On many of his coins he is shown holding a wine cup in his hand.

The person who had most influence over Jehangir was his favourite wife Nur Mahal (Light of the Palace), or, as she was afterwards called, Nur Jehan (Light of the World). She was a Persian of a good but poor family. Jehangir had seen her at the court of his father and wished to marry her but his father Akbar had not allowed him to do so and she had married Sher Khan, one of the court nobles. After her husband's death Jehangir, who had never forgotten his love for her, asked her to marry him and at last she consented. She was not only beautiful but wise and her husband consulted her in everything. Both Jehangir and his wife were very fond of that most beautiful province in the Mogul Empire — Kashmir — and they used very often to spend the hot weather in its cool climate. We can still see the beautiful gardens that the Emperor laid out in Kashmir to please his wife and they are very lovely even to this day. Nur Jehan did not like her husband's eldest son Prince Khurram and tried to prevent his becoming emperor. But a rebellion broke out and the leader of it, Mahabat Khan, one of Jehangir's generals, captured the Emperor in 1626. Then Nur Jehan showed her cleverness. She joined her husband in his captivity and won over most of the rebels to their side so that they became free once more.

In 1627 Jehangir died in Kashmir. His body was taken to Lahore and buried in a beautiful tomb at Shahdara. Near it is the tomb of Nur Jehan, who died some years after her husband, and also that of her brother Asif Jah who was the Chief Minister of the Emperor.

During the reign of Jehangir we hear first of the English in India. The East India Company, which had started in 1599, had opened a trading port at Surat in 1611 and was doing business there. But they had to pay heavy bribes to the local Governor to be allowed to trade and so one of their sea captains, William Hawkins, visited the court of Jehangir to try and get permission for the Company to trade freely. He was not able to do this because the Portuguese, who were jealous of the English and wanted to keep all the trade in their own hands, persuaded the Emperor not to grant permission.

Photo. Johnston and Hoffman, Calcutta.

THE TAJ MAHAL.

Then in 1615 King James I. of England, who had heard of the great splendour of the Mogul Emperors, sent a regular ambassador, Sir Thomas Roe, to the court of Jehangir and he was successful in obtaining the permission to trade from the Emperor.

Both of these Englishmen wrote an account of their journey and of what they saw at the Emperor's court. Sir Thomas Roe tells us a great deal about it because he stayed nearly two years.

He tells us of the magnificent processions and feasts and of the great rejoicings upon the Emperor's birthday. On that day the Emperor was weighed in a pair of golden scales and his weight, in gold, silver, jewels and many other valuable things, was given away to the people.

CHAPTER XV.

SHAH JEHAN (1627–1658).

Shah Jehan—Conquests in the Deccan—Splendour of Shah Jehan's Court—Shah Jehan, a great Builder—French visitors to the Court of Shah Jehan—The Dutch in India—The last days of Shah Jehan.

Prince Khurram, who became Emperor on his father's death, took the title of Shah Jehan (Emperor of the World). He had several brothers who also claimed the throne but he overcame them all and put them to death. Before he became Emperor he was not popular, as he was cold and stern, but after his accession he became a wise and kindly ruler and was much loved by all his subjects. Like his grandfather Akbar, Shah Jehan took Hindus as well as Mahomedans into his service. During his reign he increased his empire by conquering some parts of the Deccan in 1636. He also invaded the kingdom of Bijapur and forced the king to pay him a huge sum of money each year (£200,000). These conquests, and all the money that came to him from his empire, which was very prosperous during his reign, made him very wealthy. Hence he is sometimes called Shah Jehan "the Magnificent." No king in India had ever lived in such a splendid way. The other Mogul Emperors had generally lived at Agra but Shah Jehan was not satisfied with the palace there and wanted something bigger and grander. So he built himself a grand new palace at Delhi by the side of the old city, which now came to be called Shahjehanabad (the city of Shahjehan). Never had so beautiful a palace been seen before in India. In the great hall of the palace was the famous peacock throne. It cost nine crores of rupees and was a mass of gold and jewels. It took its name from the jewelled peacocks with which it was adorned. Upon the throne the Emperor used to sit when holding his durbar.

But the palace at Delhi is not the most famous of the buildings of the great Emperor. He had a wife called Mumtaz Mahal (Light of the Palace) whom he loved very dearly. When she died he determined to build a tomb for her, more magnificent than any which had ever been seen before. And so the wonderful Taj Mahal at Agra came to be built. It was designed by an Italian and was finally completed in 1648. This beautiful building is one of the wonders of the world. It is built of pure white marble and stands in a beautiful garden. Perhaps it looks best when we see it by moonlight. Besides the Taj Mahal, Shah Jehan also built the beautiful Moti Musjid (Pearl Mosque) at Agra.

Like his father, Shah Jehan was very fond of Kashmir and often went there to escape the heat of the summer. Here too he went on with his work of building, of which as we have seen he was very fond. In Shalimar Bagh, one of the beautiful gardens which his father had made, he built a lovely summer house of black marble.

Several travellers from Europe visited India during his reign and from two of them, the Frenchmen Bernier and Tavernier, we learn much about the splendour of the court of the Emperor.

By the time the English East India Company had greatly increased its trade and had several other trading stations in India, besides the original settlement at Surat. Another European nation, the Dutch, had also begun to trade in India. The Dutch were bold and clever sailors and soon became great rivals of the English company.

When Shah Jehan grew old his four sons began to quarrel among themselves, for each of them wanted to succeed his father as Emperor. Finally they began actual fighting. In 1658 one of them, Aurungzeb, overcame his brothers and took his father prisoner. He then became Emperor. Poor old Shah Jehan lived for seven more years but all the time he was kept a prisoner at Agra. It was a sad ending to such a splendid reign.

Photo. Bourne and Shepherd, India.

SHAH JEHAN.

CHAPTER XVI.

AURUNGZEB (1658-1707).

THE LAST OF THE GREAT MOGULS.

Aurungzeb—A strict Mahomedan—His mistaken policy—The Deccan and the Far South—The battle of Talikot—Sivaji—Aurungzeb's wars in the Deccan.

Aurungzeb, on becoming Emperor, took the title of Alamgir (Compeller of the World). His reign is a very long one, nearly 50 years, and for the greater part of it he was busy fighting. He was a strong and a great ruler but he had one great fault. The emperors who came before him were of course Mahomedans, but they had not interfered with the Hindu religion at all and, indeed, as we have seen, had many Hindus in their service. But Aurungzeb was so pious a Mahomedan that he hated every other religion except his own. This led him to interfere with the religion of the Hindus and to treat them unjustly. The result was that they lost their old friendly feeling towards their rulers and many rebellions broke out which in the end caused the fall of the Mogul Empire. Aurungzeb began to destroy the Hindu temples and to build up mosques upon their ruins. Then he started again the Jaziya tax, which the Hindus hated and which the other emperors had been too wise to collect. This caused a rebellion among the Rajputs. The rebellion was put down, but from this time the Rajputs no longer served the Emperor faithfully as they had done in the past. The time was coming when the Emperor would need their help, for new enemies were arising in the South.

Let us turn to the South of India and see what had taken place there.

In the extreme South, still lay the great Hindu kingdom of Vijayanagar of which we have read in an earlier chapter. North of this had been the Bahmani kingdom but this had broken up many years before into a number of smaller kingdoms. Two of these had become extremely powerful. These were Bijapur and Golkonda.

In 1565, the king of Bijapur had defeated the king of Vijayanagar at the battle of Talikot and from that time his kingdom had grown till it became the most important in the south of India. We have heard how the Emperor Shah Jehan made war upon Bijapur and how he had forced that country to pay him tribute. Many beautiful buildings remain to-day which show us what a powerful state Bijapur must have been. One of the provinces of the kingdom of Bijapur was the district round Poona. At the time that Aurungzeb became Emperor, the governor of this district was a man called Shahji Bhonsla and his son was the famous Sivaji.

Photo, Johnston and Hoffman, Calcutta.

MOTI MUSJID.

Sivaji and his family belonged to the people called Mahrattas. They lived in the hilly districts round Poona and also along the neighbouring coast which is called the Konkan. They were Hindus by religion and were a brave, hardy race, and very skilful horsemen. Sivaji grew up among these warlike people and gradually they began to acknowledge him as their leader. After a time he was strong enough to attack the kingdom of Bijapur. He was so successful that the king of Bijapur agreed to pay him a certain sum of money—called 'chouth'—every year, on condition that Sivaji kept quiet and did not attack him. Then Sivaji, who loved fighting, attacked the city of Aurungabad which belonged to the Emperor Aurungzeb. The Emperor, in great anger, sent an army against him and, although the Mahrattas were not defeated, Sivaji thought it wiser to give in. And so when Aurungzeb invited him to come to Delhi, he agreed to do so. But when he was in Delhi, Aurungzeb, instead of treating him honourably and making him his friend, tried to make him a prisoner. But Sivaji cleverly managed to escape and went back to his own people, full of rage against the Emperor. From that time he became a bitter enemy of Aurungzeb. In 1671 he plundered the city of Surat and soon afterwards he actually defeated the army of the great Emperor in a pitched battle. In 1680 Sivaji died, but the work that he had begun was carried on by his successors. Before he died he had really become the ruler of the Mahratta country.

In 1680 the Emperor Aurungzeb started on the long series of wars which took up the whole of the last thirty years of his reign. The Emperor hated the kings of Bijapur and Golkonda, the two Deccan kingdoms, for although they were Mahomedans, they belonged to a different sect* from himself. And so he determined to march against them and at the same time to punish the Mahrattas. And so a great army marched from Delhi and the long war began. The Emperor himself marched against Bijapur and Golkonda while his sons attacked the Mahrattas.

After a long siege Aurungzeb captured Bijapur (1686) and then he turned against Golkonda, in 1687. Here too he met with a brave resistance. King Abdul Hasan and his soldiers fought on and on, but at last the city fell by treachery.

In the meantime the Emperor's armies were attacking the Mahrattas. But the Mahrattas were not easy to attack. They avoided fighting regular battles and only attacked the Emperor's troops when they found them in small numbers. When a large army attacked them, they galloped swiftly away and it was very difficult to pursue them. And so the long war went on. In 1689 Aurungzeb captured the Mahratta leader Sambhaji, the son of the great Sivaji, and put him to death. But the Mahrattas still remained unconquered. At last in 1707, Aurungzeb, now a very old man, gave up the war in despair. The long war

Photo. Bourne and Shepherd, India.

AURUNGZEB.

had exhausted his armies and everywhere rebellions were breaking out against his rule. The Rajputs, who had not forgotten his treatment of them, rose against him. In the Punjab the Sikh power began to rise. Finally the Emperor retired to Ahmednagar, a worn out, broken man and there in 1707 he died—the last of the great Mogul Emperors.

CHAPTER XVII.

THE DECLINE AND FALL OF THE MOGUL EMPIRE.

Bahadur Shah—The Sikhs—Jahandar Shah—Farukhsiyar—Mahmud Shah—Break-up of the Mogul Empire—Growth of Mahratta power—Invasion of India by Nadir Shah—First invasion of Ahmed Shah Durani—Second invasion of Ahmed Shah—Third invasion of Ahmed Shah—Fourth invasion of Ahmed Shah—The Third battle of Panipat—Condition of India under Aurungzeb's successors.

Upon the death of Aurungzeb his eldest son, Prince Muazzim, became Emperor with the title of Bahadur Shah. There was much work for the new Emperor to do. As we have seen in the last chapter, before the death of the old Emperor, rebellions had broken out in different parts of the Empire. So the new Emperor gave up the idea of conquering the Mahrattas and went north to try and restore order. He managed to make the Rajputs his friends again and then marched into the Punjab, where there was a terrible scene of disorder. This was due to the Sikhs whom we mentioned in the last chapter.

The Sikhs—the word literally means "disciples"—were a Hindu religious sect which had been founded in the fifteenth century by a great preacher Guru Nanak. Nanak taught that there was one God before whom all men were equal. He hated cruelty of every kind and preached that all men should love one another. He had many followers and after his death his teaching was carried on by nine Gurus who followed one after another. One of these, Guru Arjun, composed the book called the Granth which contains the sayings of the Gurus and is the sacred book of the Sikh religion. Under the earlier Mogul emperors the Sikhs had been a quiet peace-loving race. But when Aurungzeb became Emperor he persecuted them very cruelly so that at last they began to rebel against him. The rebellion was put down and Teg Bahadur, the ninth Guru, was put to death.

But his son Gobind Singh, the tenth and last Guru, taught the Sikhs that they must now become fighting men to protect themselves and their religion. It was he who gave them the name of Singh (lion) and told them to let their hair and beard grow long. Under him the Sikhs became a powerful fighting force and in the last years of Aurungzeb they raised a great rebellion in the Punjab. Guru Gobind Singh died in 1708 but his successors went on fighting.

When Bahadur Shah became Emperor he marched against them and began to put down the rebellion. The Sikhs fought bravely but they were gradually beaten and driven away into the hills. But they were still a people and we shall hear a great deal more of them in later years.

While Bahadur Shah was still busy in restoring order in his Empire, he died in 1712. His son, Jahandar, succeeded him but was murdered after a reign of only one year. His successor, Farukhsiyar, was a lazy, incompetent man and he too was murdered after a reign of six years (1719), and was succeeded by Mahmud Shah.

During these years the great Mogul Empire began to break up. It needed strong and able rulers to keep it together and, when the emperors became weak and lazy, the great nobles became too powerful and began to try and make kingdoms for themselves. We have seen how the Mogul Empire had been divided into provinces ruled over by governors appointed by the emperor. Now, under weak emperors, these governors began to declare themselves independent and behave like real kings.

In 1722 Asaf Jah, governor of the provinces of the Deccan, set himself up as a separate ruler with the title of Nizam and, soon after, the governor of the province of Oudh declared himself ruler or Nawab of Oudh. In the same way, a little later on, the governor of Bengal, Ali Verdi Khan, became the Nawab of Bengal. In name, these rulers were still the servants of the Emperor at Delhi but as time went on they took less and less notice of him.

During all this time the Mahratta power had been steadily growing. The whole Mahratta people were ruled by a number of different chiefs, the leader of whom was called the Peshwa or Prime Minister.

The first three Peshwas, Balaji Visvanath, Baji Rao and Balaji Baji Rao, were very able men.

Gradually they extended their power, for they were considered such brave soldiers that no one dared to fight against them. They began to collect tribute (chouth) from the neighbouring provinces — Gujerat, Malwa and part of the Deccan. In 1738 they had become so strong that they advanced right up to Delhi itself and forced the Emperor to give up to them all the lands between the Nerbudda and Chambul rivers.

While the Mahrattas were thus attacking and weakening the Empire on the South, a new and terrible enemy appeared in the North. This was the famous Nadir Shah, the ruler of Persia.

In 1738 this great soldier conquered the province of Kabul and then suddenly crossed the Indus and invaded India. The Empire was taken by surprise and was too weak to resist. There was a battle at Karnal, close to Delhi, which was easily won by Nadir Shah, and the Emperor after the battle gave himself up as a prisoner. Nadir Shah then entered Delhi. At first the people submitted quietly but afterwards they rose against his army. Then Nadir Shah ordered the city to be plundered. Many thousands of people were put to death and all the treasures of the city were carried off. It is said that nearly £30,000,000 was taken away by the conquerors. Among other things the famous peacock throne of Shah Jehan, which was said to be worth £6,000,000, was carried off to Persia. Ten years later, in 1748, came another great invasion of India from the North. After the death of Nadir Shah, the Afghan states which he had conquered had been combined into one kingdom by an able soldier called Ahmed Shah Durani. In 1747 he invaded and conquered part of the Punjab and then advanced against the Emperor Mahmud Shah who was waiting for him at Sirhind. In the battle which followed the Afghans were defeated and driven away with great loss.

Soon after this the Emperor, Mahmud Shah, died (1748) and was succeeded by his son the Emperor Ahmed Shah. In 1752 Ahmed Shah Durani again invaded India and the Mogul Emperor was obliged to hand over the Punjab to him. Two years later the Afghans were for a short time driven out of the Punjab. The Emperor Ahmed Shah was deposed, being succeeded by the Emperor Alamgir II. (1754).

Once more (1756) Ahmed Shah Durani invaded India and once more the city of Delhi was sacked and plundered. But on the departure of the Afghans the Emperor, or rather his Chief Minister, Ghazi-ud-din, called in the help of the Mahrattas. With their help part of the Punjab was reconquered from the

Afghans once more. The Mahrattas now seemed as if they were about to found a Hindu Empire in India once more. The Emperor Alamgir II. was murdered and his successor fled to Bengal. The Mahrattas held Delhi and were really the rulers of Northern India. But Ahmed Shah Durani came back in 1761 and a great battle was fought at Panipat, the scene of many earlier battles in Indian history. In this great battle Ahmed Shah was victorious over the combined Mogul and Mahratta armies. The victory was a most important one, for it broke the power of the Mahrattas in Northern India. Had they won the battle they would probably have set up a Hindu Empire at Delhi.

If we look at a map of India at this time we shall see what great changes have taken place since the death of Aurungzeb. The old Mogul Empire is gone. It is now only a small piece of territory round Delhi. Bengal, Oudh and the territory of the Nizam are separate states, though still in name subject to the Emperor at Delhi. In the North, the Afghans held the whole of the Punjab and Scind. In the centre, the great Mahratta confederacy, composed of many divisions under powerful chiefs, such as the Gaekwar, Scindia, and Holkar—all of them under the leadership of the Peshwa—hold the country. On the coast we see the trading ports and territories of the English and French settlers which are now rising into importance. It is with the rise of these European settlements that we must deal in our next chapter.

CHAPTER XVIII.

THE RISE OF THE EUROPEAN SETTLEMENTS.

THE FRENCH AND ENGLISH IN THE SOUTH.

Early English and French Settlements in India—Struggle between the English and the French in the South—Wars in the Karnatic—Dupleix—Clive—Siege of Arcot—Battle of Wandewash.

We have seen, in an earlier chapter, how the Portuguese, the English and the Dutch had established trading stations in various parts of India. Since that time the Portuguese had become very much the weaker, and the principal part of the trade had passed into the hands of the English and the Dutch.

The first English trading port had been started at Surat in 1612, but since that time the East India Company had secured many other stations for trade upon the coast of India. In 1611 the first settlement in the South, at Masulipatam, was opened. Soon after this, in 1639, a new settlement was started on the south-east coast of India, which was called Fort St. George but which afterwards came to be better known as the town of Madras. In Bengal the English Company had opened settlements on the river Hughli in 1640, and in 1686 they bought some land upon the river and built a settlement called Fort William which came in time to be known as the

See p. 50. Photo. Johnston and Hoffman, Calcutta.

BOLI GUMBAZ, BIJAPUR.

town of Calcutta. The founder of this great city was an Englishman called Job Charnock. The Dutch too had a settlement upon the Hughli called Chinsurah. On the west coast also the English had increased their settlements. In 1661 Charles II., King of England, had married a Portuguese princess and, as part of her marriage portion, the Portuguese handed over the island of Bombay to the English and the new settlement soon became a place of great importance.

In the meantime another European power had started trading settlements in India. This power was France. France in the 17th century was ruled over by a very great king, Louis XIV., and the country was very powerful indeed. In 1664 the French East India Company had been founded and had obtained its first settlement in India at Surat in 1667. Later on, under a great and capable Frenchman called Martin, the French Company had also obtained lands on the south-east of India near the English settlement of Madras. This new settlement was called Pondicherry. The French Company had also a settlement on the Hughli which was called Chandernagore. So that in nearly every place the ports of the English and French companies stood side by side. Gradually these companies became more and more wealthy and powerful until nearly all the European trade was in their hands.

In the earlier days the two Companies occupied themselves entirely with trade and interfered hardly at all with the affairs of the country itself. But as time went on the French Company began to interfere and when disputes broke out between the rulers of the different parts of India they began to take one side or the other. Both the English and French Companies had now begun to keep a small number of troops to protect themselves.

In 1742 the famous Frenchman Dupleix came out to India as Governor of the settlement at Pondicherry. Dupleix had been in India before and had made up his mind that he would win a great Empire for France in India, if he could get the chance.

In 1743 a war broke out in Europe between England and France, called the War of the Austrian Succession. This war extended to the English and French possessions all over the world and, when the news of it reached India, the English in Madras made an attack upon the French in Pondicherry. This attack was defeated and then Dupleix marched against Madras and captured it. But now the Nawab of the Carnatic, in whose territory the towns of Madras and Pondicherry were situated, ordered the two Companies to stop fighting and said that Madras must be given back to the English. When Dupleix refused to do this, he sent an army against him. Although Dupleix's army was much smaller than that of the Nawab, the latter was utterly defeated in

Photo. Bourne and Shepherd, India.

DUPLEIX.

the battle of San Thomé (1746). This battle greatly astonished the people of India. Up to this time they had only seen the European settlers as traders and did not believe they could fight at all. But now a small army of Europeans had defeated a much larger army of Indians. The victory also encouraged Dupleix in his scheme of founding a great French Empire in India. In 1748 peace was made between England and France and Dupleix had to give back Madras to the English.

But in 1749 Dupleix saw a chance at last of really interfering in affairs in India and carrying out his plans of conquest. The great Nizam-ul-Mulk (whom we have heard of in an earlier chapter as Asaf Jah), who had practically made his province into a separate kingdom, died, having appointed his grandson Muzaffar Jung as his successor. But the Nizam had a son named Nazir Jang who wanted to be his successor also. At the same time one of the smaller divisions of the province—Arcot—was governed by a ruler named Anwar-ud-din. The ruler of Arcot before him had been a man called Dost Ali who had a son-in-law named Chanda Sahib, who wanted to be ruler of Arcot in place of Anwar-ud-din.

So Dupleix made up his mind that he would make an agreement with Muzaffar Jung and Chanda Sahib to help them to get what they wanted. Then he hoped that if he was successful he could make them do what he wanted and so the French would become the chief power in Southern India, and perhaps afterwards in all India.

So the French army, under a very good general called de Bussy, marched off to help Chanda Sahib against Anwar-ud-din. A battle took place in which Anwar-ud-din was killed (1749) and his son Mahomed Ali escaped to Trichinopoly. And now Nazir Jung came with his army against the French and Muzaffar Jung. In the meantime Mahomed Ali had sent to the English to ask for help. The English sent a small force to Nazir Jung under Major Stringer Lawrence, who is sometimes called the father of the Indian Army because of his skill in training and leading Indian troops. Nazir Jung was successful at first but after some fighting he was murdered by some of his own followers and Muzaffar Jung became ruler in his place. So that both he and Chanda Sahib had obtained what they wanted. But while he was on his way to his kingdom he was murdered. The French General de Bussy who was with him made his son Salabat Jung ruler in his place. The French were now getting very powerful in Southern India, for the new Nizam whom they had appointed would not dare to disobey them.

In the meantime Mahomed Ali was still in Trichinopoly and Chanda Sahib made up his mind to go and attack him with the help of the French. The English sent some troops to Mahomed Ali's help but they had no success till a new leader suddenly appeared. This new leader was the famous Robert Clive. Clive was a young officer, in the service of the East India Company, who had come out to India to fill up a post in the Company's offices. But he hated office work and as soon as the fighting began he had volunteered to go and serve with the troops. He now offered to take a small force and attack Arcot, Chanda Sahib's capital, in the hope that this would bring Chanda Sahib back from Trichinopoly. And so he started on his daring journey. He managed to seize Arcot and was then besieged there. After a wonderful siege of fifty days—in which Clive had only 500 men against the many thousands of Chanda Sahib—help came and then the victorious English marched to the help of Mahomed Ali in Trichinopoly. Chanda Sahib and the French were utterly defeated at Srirangam (1752) and again in the next year. Dupleix's great plan had failed. The directors of the French Company in France were dissatisfied with all this fighting and Dupleix's enemies made things worse. In 1754 he was recalled to France.

Count Lally who came out as Governor in 1756 had been a brave soldier in his youth but he was now old and he had no knowledge of India. In 1756 another war, called the Seven Years' War, broke out between England and France. Once more the

English and French fought in India and once more the French besieged Madras. But this time they did not capture the town and soon afterwards the French were utterly defeated at Wandewash (1760) by the English army under a clever General called Sir Eyre Coote. This battle ended the French Empire in India. One by one all their settlements fell into the hands of the English and finally Coote captured Pondicherry (1761). They had lost all their power with the Nizam also, as Lally had foolishly recalled de Bussy who had been living at the Nizam's court and who had great influence over him. Although the French got back their settlements when peace was made in 1763, they never had any real power in India afterwards. We must now see what had been happening to the European settlements in Bengal during these years.

CHAPTER XIX.

THE ENGLISH IN BENGAL.

Suraj-ad-daulah, Nawab of Bengal—'Black Hole' of Calcutta—Clive and Watson—Capture of Chandernagore—Battle of Plassey—Mir Jafar—Defeat of the Dutch.

We have seen in an earlier chapter how the European trading companies had established their settlements upon the river Hughli in the province of Bengal. Bengal was still in name a province of the Mogul Empire, but, as that empire became weaker, the Nawab of Bengal became more and more independent. In 1756 the ruling Nawab, Ali Vardi Khan, died. He had ruled Bengal for a great many years and was a wise and able man who kept the peace in his province and maintained good order. He had not interfered with the European settlements at all, but had allowed them to carry on their trade quite freely.

Upon his death his grandson, Suraj-ad-daulah, became Nawab. Suraj-ad-daulah was one of those people about whom it is very hard to say anything good. He was greedy, he was cruel and he was a coward.

No sooner did he become Nawab than he began to interfere with the English settlement at Calcutta. To protect themselves against attack the English had begun to make some fortifications round their settlement and the Nawab ordered these to be destroyed and when the English refused he marched upon Calcutta. The garrison was very weak and could not resist him. Many of the English managed to escape by the river but 146 of them were taken prisoners by the Nawab. These he ordered to be shut up in a small room in the fort—a room which has become famous in history as the Black Hole. It was barely twenty feet square and had very few windows. And in this dreadful place, through the heat of a June night, the poor prisoners were shut up. In the morning only 23 of them came out alive. The remainder had died during the night. When the news of this terrible act of cruelty reached Madras, an expedition was sent to punish the Nawab. The leader of this army was Clive and with him came an English fleet under Admiral Watson. The expedition sailed up the river Hughli and attacked the forts and then recaptured Calcutta. But Clive made up his mind to punish the Nawab still further and so he attacked and captured the city of Hughli. Soon after this the Nawab, who was getting frightened, offered to make peace and a treaty was signed by which he promised to give back all the property he had stolen from Calcutta. He also promised to allow the East India Company to carry on their trade without interference and to build fortifications to protect their settlement.

But the Nawab was not to be trusted. He hated the English and made up his mind to try and get the French to help him. But before he could get any help from them, the English—who were at war with the French in Europe at this time—attacked and took Chandernagore, the French settlement on the Hughli.

Clive now made up his mind that the only way to maintain order was to turn out Suraj-ad-daulah and make someone else Nawab in his place. So he entered into a secret agreement with Mir Jafar, one of Suraj-ad-daulah's generals and the brother-in-law of Ali Verdi Khan, by which Mir Jafar was to be made Nawab in place of Suraj-ad-daulah.

After this Clive led his army against the Nawab. Suraj-ad-daulah was at Plassey with 50,000 infantry, 18,000 cavalry, and 53 guns. Clive had only 900 English soldiers, and 2,100 sepoys and a few guns. Indeed the difference between the two armies was so great that even Clive, daring as he was, hesitated to advance. Then he called a council of war to decide what was to be done. In this council even Clive voted against fighting. But after some thought he decided that it was best to fight after all and so he ordered his army to cross the Ganges and, on June 23rd 1757, the famous battle of Plassey took place. The battle began by the guns of the Nawab bombarding Clive's army which had taken up its position in a mango grove. But this did little harm and, when the Nawab's troops advanced to the attack, they were driven back by heavy fire. Suraj-ad-daulah, who was a thorough coward, now fled from the field and Clive's army moved forward and put the enemy to flight.

Clive then marched to Murshidabad and appointed Mir Jafar ruler of Bengal, Behar and Orissa. Suraj-ad-daulah was captured and put to death. By a treaty between Clive and Mir Jafar the land round Calcutta was handed over to the Company and the new ruler promised to pay a large sum of money to the Company in return for the expenses they had incurred.

As Mir Jafar was unable to raise this money he had to hand over the revenues of part of his province to the Company, and their power was further strengthened by this.

By the same treaty the English Company had agreed to support Mir Jafar in case of war and the latter was now attacked by the Nawab of the neighbouring province of Oudh, who marched into Behar and laid siege to Patna. Clive marched against him but the Nawab retired at once and Clive then returned to Calcutta.

On his arrival he found a new danger had arisen. The French power in Bengal had been broken but there was still another European power left. The

Dutch — whose settlement in Bengal was at Chinsurah on the Hughli — had grown jealous of the successes of the English Company and formed a plan to attack Calcutta with the help of a Dutch fleet which had just arrived. Clive determined to strike at once. A force under Colonel Forde attacked the Dutch army near Chinsurah and completely defeated it, while the few English ships in the river fought a battle with the Dutch fleet and sank or captured nearly all the ships of the enemy. With this victory the Dutch power disappeared and the English Company were left undisturbed in Bengal.

Soon after this, in 1760, Clive went to England on leave. He had done a very great deal in a very few years. Under his leadership the English, instead of merely holding a trading port upon the river Hughli, had become the real rulers of the province of Bengal. The Nawab dared not disobey them and every year their power and wealth were becoming greater and greater.

CHAPTER XX.

CLIVE'S WORK IN BENGAL.

Mir Kasim, Nawab of Bengal—War between Mir Kasim and the English—Battle of Buxar—Clive's Return to India—Grant of the Diwani of Bengal—Clive's Reforms—His Return to England—His Work in India.

After Clive's departure the English settlement in Bengal was placed under the direction of Mr. Vansittart. No sooner had he taken office than trouble arose in the North of Bengal. This trouble was caused by the Emperor, Shah Alum, who had succeeded his father Alamgir II. Shah Alum determined to try and reconquer Bengal. So with the help of the Nawab of Oudh he led an army into the country, in 1760. The army of Mir Jafar, under his only son and a small body of the Company's troops, advanced to meet him and defeated and drove him away. Soon after this victory the tent of Mir Jafar's son was struck by lightning and he was killed. The death of his only son so affected the mind of the old Nawab that he became quite unfit to rule and so the English decided to persuade him to retire and his son-in-law, Mir Kasim, became Nawab in his place.

Mir Kasim was a strong and able ruler and introduced many reforms into his country. But although at first he was friendly with the English, a quarrel soon arose between them on a question of trade.

Photo. Bourne and Shepherd, India.

ROBERT CLIVE.

The English Company had the right to carry on its trade without paying any duty. But the officers of the Company had started increasing their own pay by taking money from the Indian merchants in return for allowing their goods to pass freely as if they belonged to the Company. The Nawab was determined to put a stop to this as he lost a good deal of money by it, and so in 1763 he did away with the customs duty altogether and so put everybody in the same position and took away the special privilege which the Company had enjoyed. This led to an open quarrel. The Nawab seized some boats belonging to the Company, and an officer of the Company named Ellis attempted to seize the city of Patna. But in this he was not successful and the Nawab now imprisoned all the English that he could lay his hands upon. In 1763 the Nawab was defeated in several battles by the English and in revenge murdered all the English prisoners whom he had taken. He then fled to Oudh to get help from the Nawab of that province. In 1764 he returned with a great army but he was utterly defeated at the battle of Buxar by the English under Sir Hector Munro. This great victory left Bengal completely at the mercy of the English and it also broke the power of the Nawab of Oudh who had come to the help of Mir Kasim. Shah Alum, the Emperor, who had also allied himself with them, found himself obliged to put himself under the protection of the victorious English.

Mir Kasim having fled, the Council at Calcutta made Nujm-ad-daulah Nawab in his place. At the same time they further strengthened themselves by taking charge of the military defence of the whole of Bengal.

Early in 1765 Clive—who was now Lord Clive—came back to India, as Governor and Commander-in-Chief in Bengal. The Directors of the Company in England were not at all pleased with the management in Bengal and they asked Lord Clive to go out again as Governor and put everything into good order.

As soon as he reached India he learned that the English army had won another victory over the Nawab of Oudh and that the latter was very willing to make peace. So Clive determined to make a settlement both with him and with the Emperor. So a meeting took place at which the Nawab of Oudh agreed to pay 50 lakhs for the expenses of the war and to allow the English to trade freely in his territory. He also had to give up the provinces of Korah and Allahabad to the Emperor, who made them over to the English to hold in his name.

The Emperor handed over the whole of Bengal, Bihar and Orissa to the English who were to pay him 26 lakhs a year in return. Thus this important treaty practically gave the English the rule of North-East India. The Nawab of Bengal still remained but all real power was taken from him by the Company who allowed him a pension of 53 lakhs.

Clive now had other important work to do. Up to this time the affairs of the Company had been managed as those of a trading company but now some arrangements had to be made for the new work of governing the province. One of the reasons why Clive had been sent out again from England was to put an end to the bribery which was going on among the Company's officers. He now held an enquiry and dismissed a number of officers who had been guilty of taking bribes, and a rule was made that all officers in future were to sign a covenant or promise that they would never accept presents of any sort.

At the same time a new Council was set up. It was to be composed of twelve members and they were to have nothing to do with the trading affairs of the Company but were simply to do their work as members of the Council and govern the country. Clive also tried to get the salaries of the officers of the Company raised so that they would not have to go in for trading on their own account. But the Directors of the Company refused to do this. While Clive was still Governor an order came out from England that the extra allowances which the army officers drew and which were called *batta* were to be stopped. This order was so unpopular that many of the officers said they would resign and the state of the army became very bad. But Clive had such great influence over the officers that in the end he persuaded them to give way. In 1767 Clive's health broke down and he returned to England being succeeded as Governor by Mr. Verelst. Clive's work in India was very great indeed. He left behind him the English rule firmly planted in Bengal and the example of honesty and justice which he had set was well followed by those who came after. The remainder of the life of this great man was saddened by sickness and by the attacks of his enemies in England. He died in 1774.

CHAPTER XXI.

HAIDAR ALI, THE LION OF MYSORE.

The Kingdom of Mysore—Haidar Ali—First Mysore War between Haidar Ali and the English.

While the English power was being firmly established in Bengal a new state was rising to power in the South of India. This state was Mysore. Mysore had been a small unimportant state governed by Hindu rulers. The man who made it powerful was Haidar Ali. He was first a common soldier and then an officer in the Mysore army. Though he was a strong, able man he had little or no education and to the end of his life could not even sign his name. Gradually he rose to the command of the army and at last he took away all the power from the Hindu Rajah and became the real ruler of the country. He trained his army with great skill till it became very strong indeed. At first his little kingdom was in great danger from the Marathas who were very jealous of Haidar Ali. But he soon found a powerful friend in the Nizam, and in 1767 the allies marched against the English settlements in Madras. The reason for war between the Nizam and the English was this. To the north of Madras there is a territory known as the Northern Cirkars and in 1765 the Emperor Shah Alum had given this territory as a free gift to the English. But the Northern Cirkars were held by the Nizam and he refused to give them up. Although an arrangement was made by which the English undertook to pay him part of the revenue of the territory, he was not satisfied and, having made an alliance with Haidar Ali, he marched against the English. But the allies were defeated in several battles by the English under Colonel Smith, and Haidar Ali then went back to Mysore. The Nizam now became very much alarmed as an English force had begun to enter his territory and in 1768 he made peace with the English.

In the meantime the English continued the war with Haidar Ali. But it was very foolishly conducted. Colonel Smith, the able leader, who had been successful in the first campaign, was recalled and another general was sent to take his place. Haidar Ali defeated him and then suddenly marched upon the city of Madras which was quite unprepared to resist him. The English were now obliged to make peace and, in the treaty which followed, both sides agreed to come to one another's help in time of war. No sooner had Haidar Ali made peace with the English than he was attacked by a large Maratha army which defeated him and besieged him in his capital, Seringapatam. Haidar Ali now sent to the English for help, as had been agreed in the treaty. But the English now refused to help him and he was obliged to make peace and to pay a very large sum of money to the Marathas. Haidar Ali never forgave the English for this and before very long they were at war with him again.

CHAPTER XXII.

WARREN HASTINGS—GOVERNOR.

Warren Hastings as Governor of Bengal—Reforms in Administration—The Rohilla War—The Regulating Act—Hastings, first Governor-General.

In 1772 there came a new Governor to Bengal. This was the famous Warren Hastings, one of the greatest Englishmen who ever came to India. He had been a member of the Council for some time and now became Governor. The Directors of the Company in England had become alarmed at the way in which so much money had been spent upon war, and they gave Hastings strict orders that he was to save as much money as possible, so that the share-holders in England might benefit. In order to do this Hastings had to carry out a good many reforms. His first reform was made in collecting the revenue. This had been collected up to this time by the Nawab, but now Hastings made a new arrangement by which it was to be collected by the Company. A number of officials were appointed, called collectors, and their duty was not only to collect the taxes in their districts, but also to act as magistrates and try cases in their courts. Hastings also set up two Courts of Appeal in Calcutta, one for civil and the other for criminal cases, in which appeals from the courts of the collectors could be heard. In this way justice could be done to everyone. Further Hastings forbade the collectors to do any other work than that of collecting taxes and hearing cases, so that they might have their whole time for their work and that it might be done quickly and thoroughly.

To help the collectors in their work as magistrates, Hastings also set up a strong police force so that good order might be kept and that an end might be made of acts of robbery and violence which were too common in those days.

Soon after Hastings became Governor trouble arose with the Marathas. We have seen, in an earlier chapter, how the Marathas had been defeated and driven away from Northern India in the great battle of Panipat (1761). But they had now become strong again and in 1770 a large Maratha army invaded Rohilkhand, a territory lying to the north of Oudh and just east of Delhi. They then occupied Delhi itself. When the Emperor, Shah Alum, heard of this he came to Delhi and was proclaimed Emperor by the Marathas in 1771. But the friendship between them did not last long. The Emperor grew weary of the greed of the Marathas and of their demands for money and offered them the provinces of Allahabad and Korah if they would go away and leave him in peace. But these provinces had been reserved for the English by the treaty which Clive had made with the Emperor after the battle of Buxar, so the English sent an army to prevent the Marathas taking them. At the same time the Nawab Wazir of Oudh, who was very alarmed at the coming of the Marathas, joined his forces to those of the English. The Marathas hesitated to attack this army and retired to their own territory. Soon after this Hastings met the Nawab Wazir at Benares and an agreement called the treaty of Benares was drawn up between them. By this treaty the English stopped paying to the Emperor, as he was now in the hands of the Marathas, the annual tribute from Bengal of 26 lacs, which they had formerly agreed to pay him. The provinces of Allahabad and Korah were to be handed over to the Nawab Wazir who was to pay the English 50 lacs a year in return. If the Marathas attacked the Nawab Wazir the English were to come to his help. There remained the question of Rohilkhand. The Rohillas could not protect themselves against the Marathas and if the Marathas conquered the country, it would be a danger to both Oudh and Bengal. So in 1774 the English and the Nawab Wazir joined their forces together and conquered Rohilkhand.

Warren Hastings did not long remain Governor of Bengal. The English Government at home had made up their minds that, as the East India Company had ceased to be only a trading company and had become the real rulers of Bengal and other parts of

Photo, Bourne and Shepherd, India.

WARREN HASTINGS.

India, it was time that the Government should have some control over its actions.

So in 1773 an act called the Regulating Act was passed by Parliament by which the Governor of Bengal became the Governor-General of all the territories in India held by the East India Company. To assist him in his work there was to be appointed a Council of four members, all of whom were to be appointed by the English Government. In this way the English Government hoped to be able to control the actions of the Company. Warren Hastings became the first Governor-General, and in the next chapter we shall deal with the events which took place during his term of office, which lasted from 1774-1785.

CHAPTER XXIII.

WARREN HASTINGS—GOVERNOR-GENERAL.

Hastings and his Council—Nanda Kumar—First Maratha War—Treaty of Salbai.

The new Governor-General soon found that, under the new arrangement, his position was very different. Although he was now Governor-General, he had actually less power than before. Three of the members of his new Council of Four came out from England and, from the very day of their arrival in India, they set to work to oppose Hastings in every way. As there were three of them, they had a majority over Hastings and the other member who usually supported him. The best known of these new Councillors was Philip Francis, a very clever man, spoiled by a fierce and ungovernable temper. From the very outset he was on bad terms with the Governor-General and on one occasion they actually fought a duel. The new Councillors began their work of upsetting all that Hastings had done, by their treatment of Oudh. As we have seen, Hastings had always kept on good terms with the Nawab Wazir and had entered into an alliance with him, as both Oudh and Bengal stood in danger from the Marathas. But when the Nawab Wazir died in 1775 and was succeeded by his son, the Council insisted on a new treaty being made by which the new Nawab had to hand over the revenues of the district of Benares and to pay the English such a large sum each year that he was practically ruined. Hastings did his best to stop this, but he could not resist the majority of the Council and the result was that, as the Nawab had no money to pay his soldiers, Oudh became so weak that it could give very little assistance to the English in the event of a war with the Marathas.

In the same year (1775) the new Councillors attacked the Governor-General himself and accused him of taking bribes. Their chief witness was a man called Nanda Kumar who accused Hastings of receiving a bribe of three and a half lacs from the widow of Mir Jaffar and who produced a letter from the Begum in support of the charge. This letter was afterwards discovered to have been forged, but the Council believed that Hastings was guilty. Then Hastings had Nanda Kumar tried on another charge of forgery and he was found guilty and hanged, as in those days by English law death was the punishment for forgery. This stern action so frightened the people that there were no more accusations made against Hastings.

Fortunately for Hastings one of the three Councillors died in 1776. This gave the control back to Hastings as there were now two on each side, and, if the votes were equal, Hastings, as Governor-General, had a casting vote.

In 1772 began the events which led up to the First Maratha War. The Marathas, who, as we have seen, had recovered a great deal of their power since their great defeat at Panipat (1761) were now a confederacy or alliance of five states—Nagpur, Holkar of Indore, Scindia of Gwalior, the Gaekwar of Baroda and the Peshwa of Poona. The Peshwa, who was the president of the confederacy, had at first been the chief minister of Satara, the kingdom of the great Sivaji, but, as years went on, the rulers of Satara became weak and the Peshwas became very powerful. In 1773 the ruling Peshwa was murdered during a mutiny of the troops in Poona and his uncle Raghoba became Peshwa. Raghoba soon afterwards led his army against the Nizam and then advanced into Mysore. While he was thus engaged he learned that a conspiracy had been formed against him in Poona by one of the ministers, an extremely clever man called Nana Furnavis, and, soon after, the widow of the late Peshwa gave birth to a son who was proclaimed as Peshwa. Raghoba at first tried to get some of the Maratha states on his side but they soon deserted him and he turned to the English in Bombay for help. By a treaty, called the Treaty of Surat (1775), the Bombay Government agreed to help him with an army of 3000 men on condition that he handed over the island of Salsette and the port of Bassein to them. The English army then advanced into Gujerat and defeated the Marathas at the battle of Arras. In the meantime the news of the Treaty of Surat reached Calcutta. The Council there did not at all approve of it and, although the Bombay Government said that the treaty had been made before the Council had been made supreme over the other Governments, ordered the war to be stopped and sent an ambassador to Poona to draw up a new treaty with the Marathas. The result of this was the treaty of Purandhar (1776) by which most of the cessions to the English were confirmed but they undertook to withdraw their troops and give no more help to Raghoba. In the meantime the Directors in England had sent out orders confirming the Treaty of Surat, and so further negotiations went on. In 1778 war broke out in Europe between England and France and, as the Government at Poona had received a Frenchman who claimed to be an ambassador from the King of France, the Bombay Government determined to take the opportunity of carrying out their agreement with Raghoba. An English force advanced to attack Poona but was surrounded at Wargaon and had to surrender, on condition that the English gave up all they had acquired since 1773.

When the news of this disaster reached Calcutta, Hastings determined to send an army across from Bengal and to take no notice of the Treaty of Wargaon. In 1780 this army under Colonel Goddard reached the Maratha territory and captured the city of Ahmedabad. A part of his army under Captain Popham marched northward and captured the famous fortress of Gwalior. This capture caused a great increase in the military reputation of the English as Gwalior was considered a very strong fortress indeed.

All through 1781 the war went on. An army came from Bombay and united with the army from Bengal and defeated the Marathas on several occasions. Both sides were now anxious for peace. The English by this time had another war to think about, as Haidar Ali of Mysore had attacked them once more. And so in 1782 peace was made by the Treaty of Salbai. The English kept the island of Salsette, but agreed to give up the cause of Raghoba who was to receive a pension. The Marathas, in return, undertook not to give any help to Haidar Ali. We must now turn to the war in the South which is called the Second Mysore War.

CHAPTER XXIV.

WARREN HASTINGS—GOVERNOR-GENERAL. (*Continued.*)

Second Mysore War—Hastings' Work in India—His Trial in England.

We have seen, in an earlier chapter, how the Madras Government had made a treaty of alliance with Haidar Ali and how, when he asked them to come to his help, they had refused to do so. The Lion of Mysore had never forgotten this and he determined that one day he would take his revenge.

In 1778 when war broke out between England and France, the Madras Government attacked and captured all the French settlements that remained. One of these was Mahé, on the south-west coast of India. When Haidar Ali heard that the English proposed to attack Mahé he was extremely angry. This was chiefly because, through the French at this settlement, he was able to get large supplies of European stores, particularly guns and ammunition. The English knew this and were all the more anxious to capture the place. So, in spite of Haidar Ali, they attacked and took Mahé in 1779. The result was that, when an ambassador came from the Marathas to ask him to join them against the English, he was only too glad to do so and in 1780 the Second Mysore War began.

Haidar Ali's army, which was nearly 100,000 in number and which had been well trained by French officers, burst into Madras, where the English had only about 8000 men to meet him, and these divided into two parts. While one part, consisting of some 2,500 men under Colonel Baillie, was marching to join the main body, Haidar Ali surrounded it at Perambukam and destroyed it. The survivors were taken to Seringapatam and thrown into prison where they were treated with great cruelty. When the news reached Calcutta, Hastings at once sent his best general, Sir Eyre Coote, to Madras with all the troops he could gather. On his arrival Coote at once marched to relieve Wandewash which was holding out bravely against Haidar's son, Tipu. Haidar Ali then attacked him with his main army at Porto Novo and a great battle took place (1781) in which Haidar Ali was thoroughly defeated.

In the next year (1782) Coote also relieved Vellore, but Haidar Ali received some French troops and a French fleet appeared off the coast under Suffren. A number of battles took place between this fleet and the English fleet under Admiral Hughes, without any great result. Soon after this the old Lion of Mysore died and was succeeded by his son Tipu. But the war still went on. Coote, broken in health, had to give up the command and the generals who took his place were not so skilful. A French general, de Bussy, of whom we have heard before, came out with some troops but did not accomplish much, as the fleet which was to support him was driven away by the English. Soon after this (1783) peace was made between England and France and so the French took no further part in the war. The Marathas had meanwhile made peace with the English. Finally, after another year's fighting, the Madras Government made a treaty with Tipu known as the Treaty of Mangalore (1784). It was a foolish peace, for Tipu hated the English and it would have been better to continue the war until he was finally crushed. As it was it took two more wars before he was conquered.

In 1785 Warren Hastings retired and sailed for England. He had been a great ruler and had done much for the country and, in spite of the accusations of bribery, he had made but little money during his term of office.

On his arrival in England he was bitterly attacked by his enemies and by many men whose minds had been poisoned against him by Francis. Finally, he was brought to trial on several charges of cruelty and corruption during his term of office as Governor-General. After a long trial, which lasted seven years, he was found to be not guilty. But he had been ruined by the expenses of the trial and was obliged to apply for a pension to the East India Company. He lived for many years and once came forward from his retirement to give evidence about Indian affairs before Parliament in 1813. He died in 1818. We know now that the charges made against him were either untrue or were made to appear much worse than they really were. But, like all great men, Hastings had enemies and for the time they almost overthrew him. Nowadays we forget his faults and we regard him as a great ruler who did much to establish the English authority in India and to give good government to many millions of people.

CHAPTER XXV.

LORD CORNWALLIS.

1786—1793.

Lord Cornwallis, second Governor-General—Tipu, the new Sultan of Mysore—Third Mysore War—The Permanent Settlement—Judicial Reforms.

The new Governor-General, Lord Cornwallis, arrived in India in 1786. He had no knowledge of India before his arrival, but he was an honest upright man and, during his term of office, several important reforms were carried out. There was also another war with Tipu, the Sultan of Mysore. Like his father Haidar Ali, Tipu was an able soldier but cruel and revengeful. As his father had been the Lion he called himself the Tiger of Mysore. We have seen how the Madras Government had made peace with Tipu by the Treaty of Mangalore (1784). But there could be no real peace with Tipu. He hated the English and made up his mind that he would do all he could to drive them out of the South of India. He began his preparations for war by trying to get the Nizam over to his side. But the latter refused to have anything to do with him, and remained faithful to his friendship with the English. Then Tipu made up his mind to fight the English by himself. So, in 1789, he began by attacking the Raja of Travancore who was a friend and ally of the

English. Lord Cornwallis at once ordered the Madras army under General Meadows to advance against Tipu. The Marathas now came forward and promised to supply some troops for the war and later in the year the Nizam also promised to help. During the first year of the war (1790) there was no great battle but several of Tipu's fortresses were taken by the English army in the South and by the Marathas in the North. In the next year (1791) Lord Cornwallis took command of the English army himself. His first success was the capture of the important town of Bangalore and then he advanced upon Seringapatam, having been joined by some 10,000 troops from the Nizam. To save his capital from attack, Tipu drew up his army to meet him at Arikera and a battle took place in which the Tiger of Mysore was badly beaten. But Lord Cornwallis was falling short of provisions and retired to Bangalore. In the following year (1792) he once more advanced with his own army and some of the troops of the Nizam and of the Marathas and reached Seringapatam. Here he was joined by an army from Bombay under General Abercrombie. Tipu now became alarmed and asked for peace and, in March 1792, he consented to a treaty by which he gave up some of his territory to the English and their allies and paid a large sum of money as expenses of the war. He also had to hand over his two sons to the English as hostages for his good conduct. This ended the Third Mysore War.

Photo, Bourne and Shepherd, India.

LORD CORNWALLIS.

Lord Cornwallis was now free to turn his attention to the government of Bengal and to carry out those reforms which give him a high place among the Governors-General of India.

The first great reform was in connection with the paying of revenue and the holding of land. The system of land-holding in Bengal was still that which had been begun under the great Mogul Emperor, Akbar. All the Zemindars or land-holders held the land from government and paid a sum of money to government for the use of the land. But, as the land was not always the same in value—as, if more work was done upon it, it naturally was worth more—the land was valued every ten years and the amount to be paid was fixed according to the value of the land. In some cases the Zemindars found that the more they improved the land the more they had to pay, so that they did not trouble themselves to improve their land. In other cases the Zemindars, in order to make more for themselves, made the ryots—the poorer class of cultivators who held land from them—pay too much rent so that much distress was caused by this. The good government of the English had caused a great increase of the population in Bengal and in order to feed this large number of people it was necessary to have as much land cultivated as possible.

So that, for all these reasons, it was time to bring in some reform. Lord Cornwallis therefore, in March 1793, introduced what was known as the Permanent

Settlement by which the Zemindars were to become the owners of the land for ever, as long as they paid an annual rent to the government, and the amount of this rent was also fixed for ever. It was also provided that the ryots should pay a fixed rent to the Zemindars and that this rent could not be altered except by the courts of law. This great settlement satisfied both parties. The Zemindars were now quite willing to open up and cultivate fresh land while the ryots felt that they were safe from having to pay too heavy a rent for their land.

The other great reform which Lord Cornwallis introduced was in the condition of the law courts. He found that the collectors had too much work to do, as they were both collectors of revenue and judges. He therefore divided up their work. In future the collectors were to collect revenue only and the only court work they were to do was to be the hearing of cases about the holding of land. To do the work of hearing other cases, he set up courts in each district in which civil cases were to be heard. If anyone wished to appeal against a judgment he could go to one of the four new appeal courts which were at Dacca, Patna, Murshidabad and Calcutta, and after this he still had the right to appeal to the Chief Court in Calcutta. At the same time courts for criminal cases were set up in which English judges sat, assisted by Hindu or Mahomedan assessors. The law of these courts was to be Mahomedan law which was slightly altered and modified.

INDIA IN 1795.

Soon after introducing these great reforms, Lord Cornwallis sailed for England in 1793. We shall hear of his return to India at a later date. Sir John Shore, a Bengal civilian, succeeded him as Governor-General.

CHAPTER XXVI.

SIR JOHN SHORE.

1793—1798.

War between the Marathas and the Nizam—Battle of Kurdla—Troubles in Oudh.

The new Governor-General was a man of peace and he determined to avoid making war if it was possible. Soon after he became Governor-General war broke out between the Marathas and the Nizam. There had been many points in dispute between them and now the Marathas demanded a very large sum of money from the Nizam. He refused to pay it and turned to the English for help. But, although the English had made a treaty with him, they refused to come to his help. In 1795 the Marathas defeated him in the great battle of Kurdla, and the Nizam was forced to agree to a peace by which he paid a very large sum of money to the Marathas and handed over some of his territory to them.

During Sir John Shore's time trouble arose in Oudh and he was forced to interfere. In 1797 the Nawab Wazir died and was succeeded by Wazir Ali who was said to be his son. But it was soon discovered that he was not the son of the late Nawab and that therefore the proper person to succeed was Sadat Ali, the late Nawab's brother. The English therefore turned out Wazir Ali and put Sadat Ali in his place. In return for this the new Nawab handed over Allahabad to the English. Soon after this Sir John Shore left India. He was succeeded as Governor-General by Lord Mornington.

MARQUESS WELLESLEY.

1798—1805.

Wellesley's Policy—Treaty with the Nizam—Fourth Mysore War—Annexations—Second Maratha War: Assaye, Argaon and Laswari.

Lord Mornington became Marquess Wellesley before he left India and he is better known by his later title. He was a very able man and was not new to Indian affairs as he had been a member of the Board of Control which, as we have seen in an earlier chapter, had been set up in England to manage Indian affairs.

As soon as he arrived in India in 1798, the new Governor-General found that Tipu, the Tiger of Mysore, had once more been plotting against the English. England and France were again at war and Tipu was anxious to get the help of the French.

For this purpose he had written to the French government and asked them to send him a large army. He had also taken large numbers of French officers into his service. Lord Mornington made up his mind to crush Tipu once and for all. But it was necessary to prepare a large army to do this. It was also necessary to make sure that the Nizam would not come to the help of Tipu. The Nizam was angry with the English because they had not helped him in his war with the Marathás, and, like Tipu, he had a large number of French officers in his service. But Lord Mornington managed to persuade him to agree to a treaty by which he was to send away all the French in his service and was not to employ any more without the permission of the English. He was to keep an army of 6,000 (this was afterwards increased to 10,000) sepoys under English officers which was to protect him from the Marathas. To pay for these troops he gave up certain territory to the English. Finally, an English officer called a Resident was to live at his court and represent the English government there. A treaty of this sort is called a subsidiary treaty. We shall hear of several more subsidiary treaties later on.

All was now ready for the war with Tipu. But the Governor-General gave him one more chance of peace. If Tipu would give up plotting with the French there should be no war. But he refused to give a clear answer and in 1799 the Fourth and last

Photo. Bourne and Shepherd, India.

MARQUESS WELLESLEY.

Mysore War began. An army of 21,000 men moved into Mysore from Madras. One of the officers of that army was the brother of the Governor-General—Colonel Arthur Wellesley, afterwards the great Duke of Wellington. Another army came down from the West. Attacked on all sides the Tiger of Mysore retreated to his capital, Seringapatam, and, on April 6th, the English army, under General Harris began the siege. Tipu offered peace but it was too late. The siege was soon over. On May 3rd Seringapatam was stormed and among the dead was found the Tiger of Mysore. He had died fighting bravely to the last. The Mysore territory was now divided up. Part was given to the Nizam and part was taken by the English. What was left, which consisted of the old kingdom of Mysore, was handed over to the real Rajah, a boy of five, descendant of the old line of rajahs who had been turned out by Haidar Ali. As a reward for the great success, Lord Mornington was made Marquess Wellesley. There was one other result of the last Mysore War and that was in the Carnatic. The government of this province had long been weak and, when Seringapatam was taken, some papers were found which proved that the Nawab had been plotting with Tipu against the English. So, when the Nawab of the Carnatic died in 1801, Lord Wellesley took the opportunity of taking over the government of the province. The Carnatic was henceforth to be part of the Presidency of Madras and the new Nawab was to receive a pension.

In the same year (1801) the English territory was extended in the North also. The province of Oudh was very weak and its weakness was a danger, as it was open to invasion by the Marathas on the south and west and on the north by the Afghans who at that time held the whole of the Punjab. Lord Wellesley tried to persuade the Nawab Wazir to strengthen himself by increasing the number of British troops in his pay. But as the latter did not wish to do this, Lord Wellesley persuaded him to sign the Treaty of Lucknow by which he handed over the territories of the Doab and Rohilkhand to the English. As this was the part of his territory most exposed to invasion the rest of Oudh was in a much safer position.

The other great event of Lord Wellesley's administration was the Second Maratha War. The power of the Peshwas had become very small and the result of this was that the great Maratha leaders were constantly at war with one another. As long as this went on there could be no real peace in India and the Marathas were a danger to all the other states. So when, in 1802, Holkar, one of the great Maratha chiefs, deposed the Peshwa, Baji Rao, and the latter appealed to the English for help, Lord Wellesley thought it a good opportunity to interfere. He therefore made a subsidiary treaty with Baji Rao, called the Treaty of Bassein, by which the Peshwa put himself under the protection of the English and received a garrison of their troops.

The great Maratha chiefs were very angry at this and gave up fighting among themselves to unite against the English and so in 1803 the Second Maratha War began. It was a great struggle. Large English armies attacked the Marathas both in the North and South. In the Deccan General Wellesley (the Governor-General's brother) took the command. On August 12th he captured the important fortress of Ahmednagar and on September 23rd he won the great victory of Assaye over the armies of the two great Maratha leaders—Sindhia and Bhonsla. It was a great victory, for Wellesley had only 4,500 men and the Marathas nearly 40,000. The English captured nearly 100 cannon and the Marathas in killed alone lost 12,000 men. Assaye is one of the great battles in the History of India. Later in the year, on November 29th, Wellesley also defeated the Marathas again at Argaon. He followed up this success by the capture, in December, of the great mountain fortress of Gawilgarh. These victories caused Bhonsla to sign the Treaty of Deogaon by which he ceded some territory, which was given to the Nizam, and promised to receive a British resident. In the meantime the English had been successful in the North. General Lake took Aligarh in August and then advanced to Delhi. Near the city he met and defeated a Maratha army and he then entered the ancient capital of India. Here still lived the Emperor, Shah Alum, old and blind, and he was now taken under the protection of the

English. Agra was taken in October, and in November Lake won the great battle of Laswari. Scindhia was now forced to make peace and in December, by the Treaty of Sirji Angengaon, he surrendered a large portion of his territory. Two of the great Maratha chiefs had thus been forced to make peace. A third, the Gaekwar, had not taken part in the war. The last remaining was Holkar who now attacked the English in 1804. He managed to defeat one English army and nearly succeeded in capturing Delhi. But his capital, Indore, was taken and he was defeated at the battle of Dig in November. Before Holkar was finally forced to make peace, the administration of Lord Wellesley was over. The authorities in England did not approve of all these wars and the expense that was caused by them and so in 1805 they sent out Lord Cornwallis again as Governor-General. Like Warren Hastings, Lord Wellesley found his policy condemned and he had to wait some years before the great work that he had done was recognized.

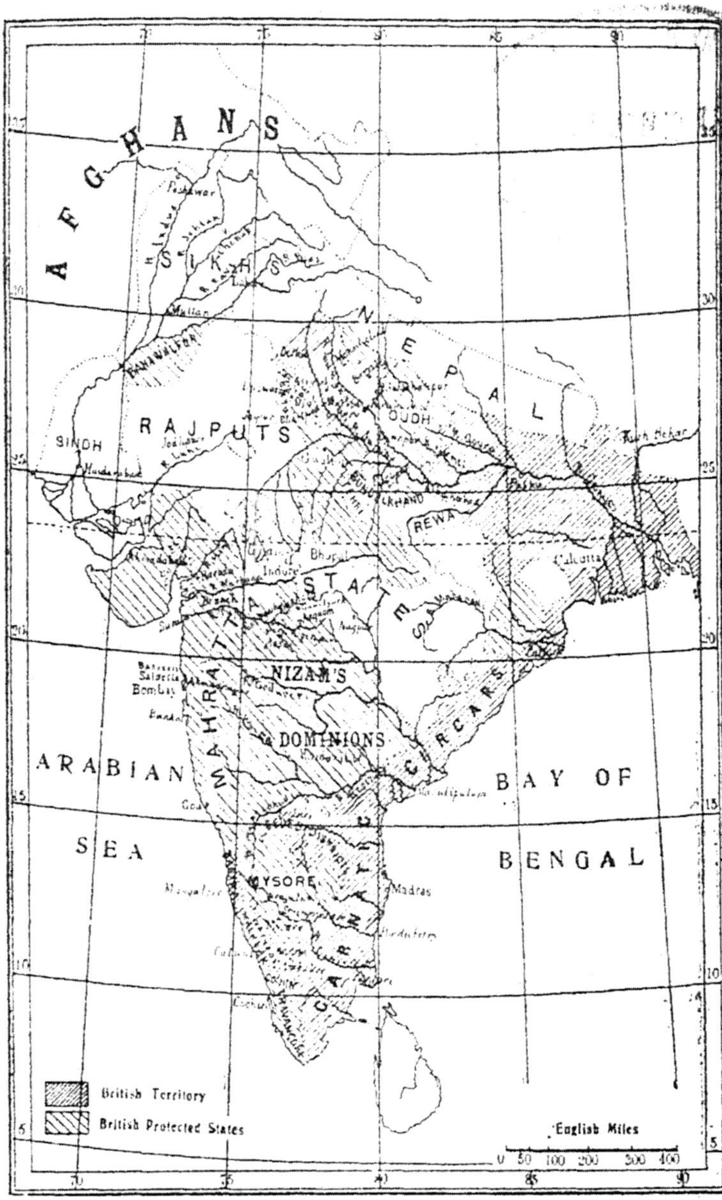

INDIA IN 1805.

CHAPTER XXVII.

LORD CORNWALLIS.

1805.

Lord Cornwallis again—Sir George Barlow—Mutiny at Vellore.

As we have seen in the last chapter, the authorities in England were not at all pleased at the great amount of money which was being spent on war. The result of these great expenses was that the profits which were made from trading were nearly all used up and so, when Lord Cornwallis came out the second time as Governor-General, he had strict orders not to make war and to let the other states in India alone. But he was now a very old man, in broken health, and, before he could carry out much he died—a little more than two months after his arrival. He was succeeded for the time being by Sir George Barlow. He too tried to carry out a policy of peace. The last Maratha chief still in arms against the English was Holkar and peace was made with him upon more favourable terms than he had a right to expect. But the policy of peace was not a success and it only prepared the way for trouble in the future. India needed one strong power to keep the whole country in order.

If there was no strong power to do this, the whole country would become a scene of disorder. While Sir George Barlow was Governor-General a serious mutiny broke out at Vellore (1806), where the family of Tipu had been imprisoned after the conquest of Mysore. It was supposed that Tipu's family had been concerned in the mutiny but it was afterwards found that they had nothing to do with it. However they were removed to Calcutta and the mutiny was put down. As a result, Sir George Barlow was transferred to Madras as Governor and a new Governor-General, Lord Minto, arrived from England, in 1807.

LORD MINTO.

1807–1813.

Bundelkhand—Embassies to Persia and Afghanistan—The Sikhs—Rise of Ranjit Singh—Treaty of Amritsar—Capture of Mauritius and Java—Abolition of the Company's Monopoly of the Trade with India.

Lord Minto had been President of the Board of Control in England and knew how anxious the authorities were not to have any more wars. But soon after his arrival he was obliged to send an army to Bundelkhand to restore order there. The chiefs of Bundelkhand were wild lawless robbers who refused to live at peace and were continually attacking and plundering the neighbouring provinces. To put a stop to this Lord Minto sent an army in 1807. The principal fortresses of these robber chiefs were captured and order was restored.

Lord Minto now turned his attention to strengthening the English position in the North by making treaties of friendship with the powers there. He was the more anxious to do this because England and France were still at war and Napoleon, who had become Emperor of the French, had sent an ambassador to Persia. The three chief powers in the North at this time were Persia, Afghanistan, and Ranjit Singh, the Sikh ruler of the Panjab.

To Persia Lord Minto sent Col. Malcolm, and after some delay a treaty was signed in 1809 by which the Persian government gave up any idea of an alliance with the French.

When we last heard of the Afghans they were in possession of the Panjab and most of the north of India. But they had been driven out by the Sikhs and their territory now only reached as far as Peshawar. The ruler at this time was Shah Shuja and to him Lord Minto sent Mountstuart Elphinstone as ambassador. This too was successful and the Afghan ruler undertook to have nothing to do with the French.

We have seen in an earlier chapter how, after the death of the last Guru, Govind Singh, the Sikhs had been almost destroyed. But about 1760 the Sikhs began to be powerful once more. They took advantage of the confusion which followed the fate of the Mogul Empire to establish themselves in the Panjab once more, and all over that province rose the castles of the different Sikh chiefs. They were constantly at war with the Afghans but, although they were beaten again and again, they were never really crushed.

Their great weakness was that they would never unite together. Instead of doing this, they formed themselves into little confederacies or leagues, each of which hated the other quite as much as they did the Afghans, and these leagues were constantly fighting among themselves. At last a leader was found strong enough to be obeyed by all. This leader was Ranjit Singh, the Lion of the Panjab as he was afterwards called. His father was the head of one of the many confederacies in the Panjab and, when he died, Ranjit Singh succeeded him (1792) though he was only a boy of twelve. His first great success was the occupation of Lahore (1799) which was handed over to him by the Afghans. He followed this up by the capture of Amritsar in 1802. The possession of the two chief cities in the province gave him great power and gradually he overcame the different Sikh leaders till all the Panjab north of the river

Sutlej owned him as its ruler. But on the other side of the river there were other Sikh states, in the province of Sirhind, and Ranjit Singh made up his mind to conquer them as well. And so in 1807 he crossed the river and prepared to attack them. But the English could not allow this, for these states were under their protection and so Lord Minto sent Mr. Metcalfe as ambassador to Ranjit Singh. After some time Ranjit Singh agreed to a treaty called the Treaty of Amritsar (1809), by which he promised to be friendly with the English and undertook not to cross the river Sutlej. The Lion of the Panjab kept this treaty faithfully, and down to his death (1839) he remained the firm friend of the English.

During Lord Minto's term of office two important places were captured by expeditions sent from India. These were Mauritius and Java.

Mauritius was the great French naval station in the Indian ocean and, as long as England and France were at war, it was always a danger to the trade of India. So Lord Minto made up his mind to capture it. In 1810 an expedition was fitted out and set off to take the island. So strong was the force that the French submitted at once and the island has ever since remained an English possession.

Java was the most important settlement of the Dutch in East Indies and, as Holland had become a part of the French Empire, it was decided to capture the island. In 1811 an expedition under Sir Samuel Achmuty successfully accomplished this object after some hard fighting. Lord Minto himself went with the expedition as a volunteer. Java did not long remain an English possession. It was given back to the Dutch at the general peace which ended the long war with France in 1815. In 1813 Lord Minto's term of office came to an end and he left for England leaving behind him a good record of order maintained during his time as Governor-General.

In his last year a great change took place in India. Hitherto the East India Company had had a monopoly of the trade with India—that is no one else was allowed to trade there at all. But when their charter, which gave them the power to govern the country, was renewed in 1813 the monopoly was done away with and trade with India was thrown open to everybody.

CHAPTER XXVIII.

LORD HASTINGS.

1813—1823.

War with Nepal—Treaty of Segauli—War with the Pindaris—Third Maratha War—Administrative Reforms—Conquest of Ceylon—Singapore acquired by purchase.

When Lord Minto left India he left behind him two questions which had to be settled, and, although Lord Moira—as the new Governor-General was called when he first came out—was anxious not to interfere with the other states he was soon obliged to do so.

The first of these questions was Nepal. Nepal was a mountainous state on the slopes of the Himalayas. In the 14th century it had been conquered by the Rajputs. The people of the country were known as Gurkhas and were a brave warlike race. They had first of all attempted to enlarge their country by conquering part of China. But when they were beaten back on that side they began to try and seize land in India. They had seized a part of the province of Oudh in the time of Lord Minto, and he had objected but the Gurkhas took no notice. In 1814 they began once more to disturb the peace of India, so Lord Moira made up his mind to go to war with them. The first part of the war was not very successful. Several armies invaded Nepal but only one of the generals, Ochterlony, showed any skill and the English were defeated on several occasions. The second campaign was more fortunate. In 1815 the Gurkhas were defeated at Almorah and General Ochterlony captured the fortress of Malaun. The Gurkhas now offered to make peace. A treaty was drawn up but, before it could be carried out, the Gurkhas changed their minds and war broke out again. This time General Ochterlony advanced against the Gurkha capital, Khatmandu. He had got within fifty miles of it when the Gurkhas, thoroughly frightened, consented to make peace. By the treaty of Sagauli (1816) they gave up the provinces of Kumaon and Garhwal to the English and agreed to receive an English resident. The Gurkhas have always kept loyally to this treaty and have always remained firm friends of the English. Some of our best regiments to-day are recruited from the hardy little men of Nepal. Lord Moira was created Marquess of Hastings for his successful conduct of the war.

The Governor-General now had to turn his attention to the other great question — the state of Central India. Here a terrible state of confusion existed. The whole country was in the hands of the Pindaris, bodies of wild irregular soldiers — little better than robbers — who were supposed to be in the service of the different Maratha chiefs. They plundered and

Photo. Bourne and Shepherd, India.

LORD HASTINGS.

burnt and ravaged the country but the English so far had not punished them. This was because the directors of the East India Company had made up their minds to have no more wars if they could possibly help it. But at last, in 1816, the Pindaris became so violent that Lord Hastings made up his mind to crush them. At the same time a new head of the Board of Control in England came into office. This was Mr. Canning, the father of a future Governor-General. He too saw that the state of disorder could not go on and so Lord Hastings was given permission to make an end of the Pindaris. In 1817 the war began. Gradually the Pindaris were surrounded on all sides by large armies and in 1818 their last leader was defeated and the war came to an end. But in the meantime trouble had arisen with the Marathas. The Peshwa and the other Maratha chiefs had encouraged the Pindaris and intrigued with them in the hope that with their help they would be able to free themselves from English control. The Peshwa began the war by attempting to seize the Resident at Poona. But an army was quickly sent and the Peshwa's forces were put to flight. The Peshwa himself fled. One by one the great Maratha chiefs were defeated. The Bhonsla of Nagpur with an army of 18,000 men was utterly crushed by a small English force at Sitabaldi, near Nagpur, and had to surrender. Holkar was defeated at Mahidpur. Both these rulers had to conclude new subsidiary treaties and place themselves under the protection of the English. Finally, the Peshwa himself surrendered. The greater part of his territory was annexed by the English and added to the Presidency of Bombay. The Peshwa himself was given a pension of eight lacs and sent to live at Bithur near Calcutta. What was left of his dominions — the state of Satara — was given to a descendant of the great Sivaji, who was made raja under the protection of the English. The whole war lasted a very short time — only four months. At the end of it order reigned in India. The Pindaris were finally crushed and the Maratha chiefs lay at the mercy of the English. The new territories had now to be organized. Fortunately, there were in India Englishmen well fitted for the work. Elphinstone, Malcolm, and Metcalfe were principally entrusted with the task. As far as possible the old Indian system was retained. The villages kept their old headmen who were responsible for order. The value of the land was estimated and the revenue fixed at a fair rate so as not to press too heavily upon the owners. Lord Hastings showed his ability in other ways than this. Vernacular schools were started under his rule and he took a great interest in education. Up to this time there had been very strict rules about the publication of newspapers. But Lord Hastings had these rules altered and it was during his term of office that the first vernacular newspaper appeared at Serampur.

The island of Ceylon came finally under British rule at this time. It had been conquered from the Dutch and handed over to England at the great peace of 1815. But the native rulers had carried on war with the British for a number of years. In 1819 this war came to an end and Ceylon became a regular possession.

We have seen how in the time of Lord Minto the island of Java had been conquered from the Dutch. At the peace of 1815 the island had been given back to them. This gave the Dutch a great hold over the trade in the East Indies and there was a danger of the English trade being shut out altogether. To prevent this, Sir Stamford Raffles, who had been Governor of Java while the English held it, suggested buying the island of Singapore at the end of the Malay peninsula. Lord Hastings carried out the plan and Raffles became the first Governor of Singapore. Under his wise rule the island became a flourishing place and it is now one of the great ports of the Empire and the meeting place of the trade of India and China. In 1822 Lord Hasting's rule came to an end and he left India for England. He had done a great work in the country but, like other great Governors-General, he received little thanks for all he had done. The directors of the Company in England thought only of their profits and did not realise how necessary it was to keep order in India with a strong hand.

CHAPTER XXIX.

LORD AMHERST.

1823—1828.

First Burmese War—Treaty of Yandabu—Storming of Bharatpur.

The new Governor-General, Lord Amherst, arrived in 1823. He had just returned from China, where he had been sent as ambassador to try and make relations with the Chinese government more friendly. As soon as he arrived in India Lord Amherst found himself faced with a war with Burma. The kingdom of Burma lay to the east of Bengal and in 1822 it had become much more powerful by the conquest of Assam and Arakan. The Burmese had always behaved in an arrogant way towards the English and, in 1818, had demanded that the whole of Eastern Bengal should be given up to them. Lord Hastings had taken no notice of this, but the Burmese now began to attack Eastern Bengal. Lord Amherst tried to keep peace but the Burmese were bent on war and in 1824 the First Burmese War broke out. An army was sent from India and took the town of Rangoon, but the heavy rains stopped a further advance for some months. In the meantime the army suffered much from fever. So bad was

Photo. Bourne and Shepherd, India.

FORT OF BHARATPUR.

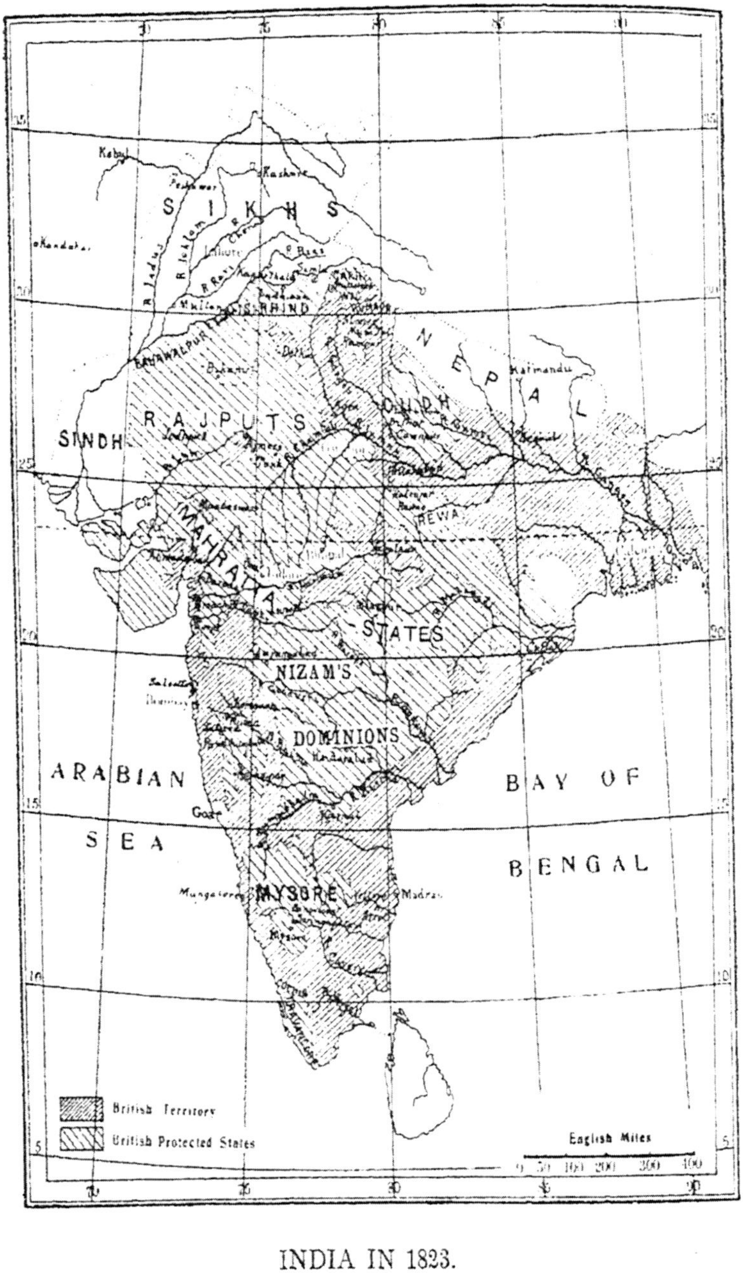

INDIA IN 1823.

the health of the troops that, when the news reached India, some regiments which were under orders to go to Burma refused to do so and broke into mutiny. One regiment actually had to be disbanded altogether. In the beginning of 1825 the war was renewed with more success. The strong position of Donabu was captured and soon afterwards Prome, the capital of Lower Burma, fell. After this success the English advanced up the river Irrawaddy and approached Ava, the capital. The Burmese king now opened negotiations for peace through some American missionaries at his court, and in 1826 the Treaty of Yandabu was signed, by which the Burmese handed over the provinces of Assam, Tenasserim and Arakan to the English and paid a crore of rupees for the expenses of the war. The other great military event during Lord Amherst's term of office was the siege of Bharatpur, the great Jat fortress in Rajputana. The old raja had died and his son had been made raja in his place and was under the protection of the English. But he was turned out by his cousin and the English were obliged to interfere. In 1826 an army of 21000 men and 100 guns attacked the great fortress. After a month's siege Bharatpur fell. The walls were thrown down and the raja was put back upon his throne.

Lord Amherst left India in 1828. It was during his time, in 1826, that Simla first became the summer capital of India.

LORD WILLIAM BENTINCK.

1828—1835.

Abolition of Sati—Suppression of the Thugs—Financial Reforms—Employment of Indians in Government Service—English Education—Renewal of the East India Company's Charter.

The new Governor-General had been in India before, for he had once been Governor of Madras. He came out from England with special orders to keep peace and save as much money as possible. This duty he carried out and we hear of no wars during his term of office. Instead we hear of many great reforms, the most important of which we must now consider.

The first great reform was the abolition of Sati. Sati was the custom, common among Hindu widows, of being burnt alive with their dead husbands. It was a cruel custom and many women suffered unwillingly but, up to this time, the Government had not interfered with it. Lord William Bentinck determined to put a stop to it altogether and, in 1829, an act was passed which forbade Sati and made those persons who allowed it to take place guilty of murder. And so the cruel custom gradually died away.

The second great reform was the suppression of the Thugs. The Thugs formed a kind of secret society of murderers and robbers who had been carrying on their horrible profession in India for years.

Their practice was to waylay travellers on the road and get them to join them. Then when the victim was quite unprepared he was suddenly seized and strangled. Hundreds of travellers died in this way every year. Soon after Lord William Bentinck's arrival the Government obtained some information about the Thugs and their organization. This led to a special department being formed to deal with them. All over India the Thugs were arrested and, while a number were put to death, a great many of them were formed into a settlement at Jabalpur, where their descendants are still living. In a few years the terror of the Thugs had quite disappeared.

Lord William Bentinck had come out, as we have seen, with orders to save money and this he did in several ways. He reduced the size of the armies in the different Presidencies and cut down the allowances to officers. He did away with some of the courts of appeal which were expensive to keep up and were not working well. Then he increased the revenue by collecting a duty on the opium grown in the different states. This opium trade had become very large as nearly all the opium went to China and the amount increased every year. But up to this time only the opium which was grown in Bengal paid duty, while much opium was grown in other parts of India. The Governor-General now decided that all opium must pay a duty and so a much larger sum of money was paid in to Government.

The revenue was also increased by the settlement of the territory near the province of Oudh. This new territory was given the name of the North-West Provinces. The land was carefully valued and the amount of taxes to be paid was fixed. In this new province, as well as in the older provinces, Lord William Bentinck introduced another great reform. Up to 1831 the people of India had practically no share in the government of the country. But from that time the system was introduced of throwing open government posts to Indians as well as to Englishmen. Two good results came from this. The Indians were pleased at getting a share in the government and, as they did not require such high salaries as the English officials, a good deal of money was saved.

Like Lord Hastings, Lord William Bentinck was much interested in education. In his time (1835) it was decided that English should be the official language, for admission into all higher, public appointments. This reform was mainly due to Lord Macaulay, the great English writer and statesman, who was at that time a member of the Governor-General's Council. During Lord William Bentinck's time the charter of the East India Company was once more renewed. We have seen how it had been renewed in 1813 and how at that time trade had been thrown open to everybody. Now it was decided that the Company should give up trading altogether. In return

Photo. Bourne and Shepherd, India.

LORD WILLIAM BENTINCK.

for this the charter was renewed for another twenty years. At the same time the privilege which the Company enjoyed of having the trade with China in its own hands was done away with and the China trade was thrown open to everybody.

Lord William Bentinck left India in 1835. He had done a great work of reform and his great efforts on behalf of the people over whom he ruled have made him one of the best remembered of the rulers of India.

CHAPTER XXX.

LORD AUCKLAND.

1836—1842.

Sir Charles Metcalfe and the Liberty of the Press—First Afghan War.

For a short time after the departure of Lord William Bentinck the office of Governor-General was held by Sir Charles Metcalfe. But he made himself very unpopular with the directors of the Company in England by bringing in a law which freed the press from all control, and, in 1836, Lord Auckland came out as Governor-General.

Lord Auckland had intended to devote himself to the peaceful progress of the country but instead of this he found himself occupied, during nearly the whole of his term of office, in a war with Afghanistan, called the First Afghan War.

The Amir of Afghanistan at this time was Dost Mahomed. He had turned out the old reigning family and its representative, Shah Shuja, was living in exile in India. In 1835 there had broken out a war between Ranjit Singh and the Afghans in which the Sikhs had conquered the province of Peshawar. The Amir had appealed to the English but the Governor-General, though he promised to send an ambassador to talk over affairs of trade, declined to interfere in the war.

In 1837 this ambassador, Captain Alexander Burnes, arrived in Kabul. Now at this time the English Government believed that both Russia and Persia meant to invade India, and when a Russian ambassador arrived in Kabul in the same year (1837) they became very suspicious.

Instead of trusting Dost Mahomed, who was anxious to be friendly with the English, Lord Auckland made up his mind that the Amir was plotting with Russia and Persia against the English, although the Persians had attacked Afghanistan and would have captured the fortress of Herat (1838) but for the bravery of an English officer, Lieutenant Pottinger, who happened to be there.

And so the Governor-General made a great mistake. He determined to join with Ranjit Singh in a war against Dost Mahomed, drive him from the throne, and put back Shah Shuja. It was a great mistake, for Shah Shuja was not liked by the Afghans and they did not want him as their ruler at all.

However the mistake was made and at the end of 1838 the expedition started. One army marched up through the Punjab, and another from Bombay came up through Sind, the chiefs of that country being forced to allow it to pass through their territory. The united armies then entered Afghanistan and Shah Shuja was proclaimed Amir at Kandahar in May 1839. After storming the strong fortress of Ghazni, the old capital of Mahmud, the army entered Kabul in August.

Part of the army now went back to India, but in order to protect Shah Shuja, a part was left in the country. Sir William Macnaghten, who had been Lord Auckland's chief responsible adviser in Afghan affairs, was left with the Amir as ambassador. In the meantime the difficulties of the English were increasing. In June 1839 Ranjit Singh, the Lion of the Punjab, died and the weak ruler who took his place was unable to keep the Sikhs in order. The Sikhs began to object to the passage of the English troops through the Punjab and to plot with the Afghans. All through 1840 the storm was gathering. Dost Mahomed himself surrendered to the English and was sent to India and given a pension. But his son, Akbar Khan, remained in the country and became the leader of the discontented party. In 1841 the Afghans rose in rebellion. Burnes, who had come back with Sir W. Macnaghten, was murdered and the English armies were shut up in the cities of Kabul and Kandahar, while a small force held Jalalabad near the Khyber pass. Macnaghten now tried to arrange a treaty with Akbar Khan by which the English should leave the country and Dost Mahomed

Photo. Bourne and Shepherd, India.

THE KHYBER PASS.

should be brought back. But he was murdered by Akbar Khan while having an interview to talk over the treaty.

The English general, Elphinstone, an old and feeble man, now agreed to leave the country with his army and, in January 1842, the whole force, about 4,500 troops, 12,000 followers, and many women and children left Kabul. It was bitterly cold weather and deep snow lay upon the ground. When the army entered the Khurd Kabul pass it was attacked on all sides. To save the women and children they were surrendered to Akbar Khan who treated them kindly. Then the army continued its dreadful journey. Man after man was killed till at last only one survivor,. Captain Brydon, reached Jalalabad with the news of the disaster. The Afghan army soon reached Jalalabad and attacked it but the garrison under General Sale resisted bravely and managed to hold out till help arrived. The other British army which was at Kandahar maintained its position.

Lord Auckland had made so many mistakes that it was quite time that a new Governor-General should take his place. In February 1842, Lord Ellenborough, arrived as Governor-General and it was during his term of office that the Afghan war was brought to an end.

LORD ELLENBOROUGH.

1842—1844.

End of the First Afghan War—Conquest of Sind—Gwalior Affairs.

The first duty of the new Governor-General was to put an end to the Afghan war. But it was first necessary to punish the Afghans for the disasters of the retreat from Kabul. An army under General Pollock moved up the Khyber pass and found the garrison of Jalalabad still holding out bravely, after a five months' siege. Pollock's army then advanced on Kabul and joined the army of General Nott which had come up from Kandahar. In the meantime the unfortunate Shah Shuja had been murdered by the Afghans themselves. After defeating the Afghan army, the English once more entered Kabul. The women and children and the other prisoners were safely recovered. As some punishment for the murder of Macnaghten and Burnes, the great bazaar of Kabul was destroyed and then the English army left the country altogether. Dost Mahomed was set free and went back to Afghanistan where he once more became Amir.

After the Afghan war the province of Sind was conquered. The Mirs or chiefs of that province had been forced to allow the English troops to pass through on their way to Afghanistan. But they became discontented at this and it became necessary to send an army to restore order. Lord Ellenborough sent General Sir Charles Napier. He defeated the armies of Sind in the battle of Miani (1843). Hyderabad was then taken and, when another army advanced against the English, it was defeated at Daba. Sind was now annexed and became part of the Bombay Presidency.

Lord Ellenborough had also to interfere in the State of Gwalior. Here a dispute as to the succession led to an outbreak which might have become dangerous. The Gwalior army was a strong one and was suspected of plotting with the Sikhs, who had become unfriendly to the English since the death of Ranjit Singh. To prevent further trouble a force under Sir Hugh Gough was sent to Gwalior. The mutinous Gwalior army was defeated at Maharajpur and Punniar and it was arranged that the state of Gwalior should maintain a much smaller army in future.

Lord Ellenborough's term of office came to an end soon after this. The government in England were afraid that he would engage in more wars which they were anxious to avoid. And so in 1844 he was recalled and was succeeded by his brother-in-law, Sir Henry Hardinge.

CHAPTER XXXI.

SIR HENRY HARDINGE.

1844—1848.

First Sikh War—Battles of Mudki, Ferozshah, Aliwal and Sobraon—Treaties of Lahore—Civil reforms.

The new Governor-General was a veteran soldier and he came to India at a time when a strong hand was badly needed. Soon after his arrival there broke out what is called the First Sikh War. The great Ranjit Singh died in 1839 and a period of confusion followed. His son, Kharak Singh, died, after a short reign, in 1840, and Nur Nihal Singh who succeeded him was killed by the fall of a gateway very soon after. Then one ruler followed another. The army, which was a very powerful one, grew very disorderly and leader after leader was murdered. Finally, having been for some time without pay, the troops demanded war with the English and, in December 1845, the Sikhs began to cross the Sutlej. The English Government had long seen that trouble with the Sikhs was certain to come and the garrisons along the frontier had been strengthened to meet the danger. As soon as the news arrived, the commander-in-chief, Sir Hugh Gough, started off with his army from Ambala.

The first battle took place at Mudki. It was long and fierce but in the end the Sikhs were defeated and driven from the field. Among the killed on the side of the English was Sir Robert Sale, the brave defender of Jalalabad in the Afghan War. In the meantime the Sikhs had formed a strong fortified camp at Ferozshah and the English advanced to attack this. At the end of a hard day's fighting (December 21st), the English had captured part of the camp but the Sikhs still held the remainder. It was a bitterly cold night and the troops suffered terribly from cold and hunger. In the morning the battle was renewed and the Sikhs were put to flight. Another Sikh army now came up but withdrew without fighting. The losses were very heavy on both sides but a great number of guns were captured from the Sikhs.

The English now had to wait for supplies and ammunition to come up from Delhi and in the meantime the Sikhs recrossed the Sutlej and attacked Ludhiana. But General Sir Harry Smith moved against them with a strong force and, at Aliwal (January 28th), they were defeated and once more driven over the river. The Sikhs now took up a strongly fortified position at Sobraon and here they were attacked by the English under Sir Hugh Gough and Sir Harry Smith. A great battle took place (February 10th) in which the Sikhs were completely defeated. Nearly 10,000 of them were killed and sixty-seven guns and a large quantity of stores fell into the hands of the English. After this great victory the English army crossed the Sutlej and advanced on Lahore, the capital, which was reached on February 20th. The Sikhs now submitted and, on February 23rd, peace was made at Lahore. The boy Dhulip Singh, who was said to be the son of Ranjit Singh, was to remain rajah, but the Sikhs had to give up all the land on the left bank of the Sutlej to the English and also the Jullandur Doab, a rich territory lying between the Beas and the Sutlej. The army was to be reduced in size and a sum of £1,500,000 paid for the expenses of the war. In order to raise this sum the Sikhs sold the province of Kashmir to Gulab Singh, the rajah of Jammu, for £1,000,000, and the English undertook to recognize him as ruler of Kashmir. His descendants are the present reigning family.

Later on it was decided that an English resident—Major, afterwards Sir Henry Lawrence—should reside at Lahore, and that an English army should remain in the country till the end of the year, to keep order.

Sir Henry Hardinge and Sir Hugh Gough were both made peers in reward for their services and so the First Sikh War came to an end.

As the time drew near for the English army to leave the Punjab the leading Sikh chiefs grew much alarmed. They saw that there was so much quarrelling among them that they could never form a good government themselves and they were afraid that, as soon as the English army left the country, there would be more disorder. And so they requested Lord Hardinge not to withdraw his troops until the young rajah should have grown up and be able to govern for himself. Lord Hardinge was not anxious to keep an army in the Punjab, but he saw that it was the only thing to be done in order to keep that province quiet. Therefore, in December 1846. a new treaty was signed by which the chiefs of the Punjab agreed that the country should be governed by a council of eight of them under the English resident. An English army was to remain in the country to keep order and the expense of this was to be met by the Sikhs themselves. It seemed a good arrangement but, as we shall see before long, it did not last.

Lord Hardinge spent two more years in India and during that time he was occupied in more peaceful ways. Large canal works were started and plans were begun for the introduction of railways into the country. The abolition of Sati was extended into the Native States and the other reforms begun by Lord William Bentinck were carried out. Lord Hardinge left India in 1848 after only four years of office. But he had done a great deal in a short time and his work was carried on by his successor — the great Governor-General — Lord Dalhousie.

CHAPTER XXXII.

LORD DALHOUSIE.

1848 — 1856.

Second Sikh War — Battles of Chilianwalah and Gujrat — Annexation of the Punjab — Second Burmese War — Annexation of Lower Burma — Doctrine of 'lapse' — Annexation of Oudh — Material progress — Renewal of the Company's Charter.

The new Governor-General was only thirty-six years old, but he had held office in the government in England and was a strong man of very great ability. His term of office is one of the most important in the history of India and much of the prosperity of the country to-day dates from his time.

Very soon after his arrival, the new Governor-General had to deal with trouble in the Punjab. The Governor of Multan, Mulraj, owed certain sums of money to the government at Lahore, and when he was called upon to pay them, he refused to do so and resigned his office. Two English officials, Vans Agnew and Anderson, and a new Governor were sent to Multan, but on their arrival they were attacked by the followers of Mulraj and murdered (April 1848). Before their death they managed to send news to Lieutenant — afterwards Sir Herbert — Edwardes who was in Bannu. Edwardes immediately collected a small force and marched on Multan.

On the way he was joined by troops from the Nawab of Bahawalpur and some other friendly native rulers and with this force he defeated Mulraj and shut him up in Multan.

An army under General Whish soon arrived and in September 1848 the siege of Multan began. It lasted until January 1849, for the fortress was a very strong one. At last the city was taken. Mulraj was captured and spent the rest of his life in prison.

In the meantime the whole of the Punjab was in rebellion and the Second Sikh War had begun.

Lord Dalhousie was not a man to waste time. In November 1848 a large army under Lord Gough entered the Punjab. After a battle at Ramnagar, in which neither side won the victory, the Sikhs took up a strong position at Chilianwalah. Here on January 13th, 1849, a great battle was fought in which the English just managed to win, though with heavy losses. As Multan had now fallen, the army of General Whish now joined that of Lord Gough and on February 27th, 1849, the united armies attacked the Sikhs at Gujrat. The Sikhs were utterly defeated and their army destroyed. The English pursued them to Rawal Pindi, when the remains of their army surrendered.

This was the end of the Punjab as an independant state. Lord Dalhousie had made up his mind that there could be only one end to the war and, on March 29th, 1849, the whole of the Punjab was annexed. The young Maharajah, Dhulip Singh, was given a pension. He afterwards became a Christian and settled in England.

The settlement of the new province was entrusted to a Board of Control of three members—the two famous brothers John and Henry Lawrence and a third member Mansel. Under their able rule the Punjab soon became a peaceful and orderly province. Roads were opened in all directions and a great system of canals was begun by means of which the drier parts of the province soon became rich and fertile. In a few years the Punjab had learnt to respect and obey its new rulers. When the great storm of the Mutiny burst in 1857, the people of the Punjab loyally supported the English and many fine regiments were formed in the province and did their duty in suppressing the rebellion. To-day the Punjab still remains one of the best recruiting grounds for the army and its soldiers have gained honour in many a hard-fought battle.

Soon after the annexation of the Punjab, Lord Dalhousie was obliged to start upon another war—the Second Burmese War. The Burmese government had learnt nothing from their defeat in the first war and treated the English merchants in

Photo. Bourne and Shepherd, India.

LORD DALHOUSIE.

Burma so badly that at last they appealed to the Governor-General. Lord Dalhousie determined to teach the Burmese a good lesson. A strong force was sent to Burma and the port of Rangoon was taken and soon afterwards Prome, the capital of Lower Burma, fell. Lord Dalhousie then announced that the whole of Lower Burma would in future belong to the English.

But it was not only by war that Lord Dalhousie increased the English territories in India. We have seen how many of the states in India had made subsidiary treaties by which they put themselves under English protection. Many of the rulers of these states did not care at all for the welfare of their people. and their territories were very badly governed. Now the custom had always been that, if a ruler had no son, he might adopt one who should become ruler after his death. Lord Dalhousie thought that it was time to break through this custom and therefore he introduced a system called the system of 'lapse.' By this system, if a ruler had no son, although he might adopt one and leave him his *private* property when he died, the state itself could not go to the adopted son but lapsed to the English Government. In this way a number of states, large and small, came into the possession of the English. Satara in 1849, Jhansi and the Carnatic in 1853, and Nagpur in the same year were some of the most important.

Lord Dalhousie's last great addition to the English territories was the province of Oudh. The state of this province had long been going from bad to worse and the Nawab had again and again been warned by the English Government. At last Lord Dalhousie decided that the only thing to do was to annex the province and, in 1856, Oudh became an English province and its ruler was given a pension for the rest of his life.

Though they had long ceased to have any power, the descendants of the Mogul emperors still kept their court in the palace at Delhi but, as this court was expensive and was a great centre for all kinds of plots, the government decided that it should come to an end on the death of the reigning Emperor, Bahadur Shah II. It was arranged that his family should give up the palace on his death but nothing was done as long as he was alive. We shall see, in a later chapter, how the presence of the old Emperor in Delhi was made use of at the time of the Mutiny.

Lord Dalhousie did not make his great name as a Governor-General merely by annexing territory. In many other ways he laboured for the good of the country. His health was very bad but he kept bravely to his duty and agreed to have his term of office made longer so that he might stay and finish his work. Railways were introduced into India in his time, and before he left the country, in 1856,

INDIA IN 1856.

many miles were being built. The railways caused a great increase in trade and busy factories sprung up all over the country. To Lord Dalhousie we also owe the introduction of the telegraph and the half-anna post. To manage all these new undertakings he organized the Public Works Department which we still have to-day. In his time also another great government department came into existence — the Department of Public Instruction. Under this department vernacular schools were opened all over the country.

In 1853 the Charter of the East India Company was renewed for the last time and several important changes took place. Competitive examinations were started for admission into the Civil and Military services. A new Legislative Council was appointed to assist in making laws, and the presidency of Bengal was put in charge of a Lieutenant-Governor, so as to give the Governor-General more time to attend to the affairs of the whole country. Lord Dalhousie gave up his office in 1856 and returned to England. He had given his life for India, for his health was utterly broken by all the hard work he had done for the good of the country. He died in 1860 when still quite a young man. India owes a good deal to this great man, one of the most just and honourable rulers who ever governed the country.

CHAPTER XXXIII.

LORD CANNING
(THE LAST GOVERNOR-GENERAL.)

1856—1858.

War with Persia—The Mutiny—Transfer of Government from the Company to the Crown—The Queen's Proclamation.

The new Governor-General was the son of a great English statesman, of whom we have heard before. Lord Canning had held some offices in the Government in England and was considered a man of sound views. When he arrived in India all seemed peaceful and yet, in a little over a year, the new Governor-General had to face the terrible crisis of the Indian Mutiny.

Before we consider the causes of that great outbreak, we must refer to a war with Persia which began in 1856. In 1855 the Persian government had so insulted the English ambassador that he had been obliged to leave the Persian capital, and they then followed this up by attacking Herat, on the border of Afghanistan. The English were therefore obliged to send an army up the Persian Gulf and Bushire was captured after some fighting. Further successes followed and, in the spring of 1857, the Persian Government was obliged to make peace

Photo. Bourne and Shepherd, India.

LORD CANNING.

and promised to let Herat alone in future. A treaty was also made with Dost Mahomad, the Amir of Afghanistan, by which both he and the English put an end to their old quarrel and the English agreed to help him if he was attacked by Persia. Dost Mahomad loyally observed this treaty of friendship to the end of his life. Two of the officers who fought in this Persian War—Sir James Outram and Colonel Henry (afterwards Sir Henry) Havelock—were to become still more famous during the great Mutiny.

We must now turn to the Mutiny itself and try and understand some of its causes. The many changes introduced by Lord Dalhousie had alarmed many inhabitants of the country. The inhabitants of the states which had come to be English by the system of "lapse" were uneasy and ready for rebellion. There was also an old prophecy, widely known among the people of India, that the Raj of the Company would last a hundred years and it was just hundred years since the battle of Plassey. The retreat from Kabul in the First Afghan War and rumours of defeats in the Crimean War (between England and Russia) which was just over, had made a great number of people think that the English power was getting weaker. The army too was not well managed. Many of the English officers were away from their regiments, doing special duty, and the Indian soldier, who likes to know and trust his officers, saw very little of them. The generals and other senior officers were many of them far too old to do their work properly. Above all this there were rumours spread all over the country that the English had made up their minds to interfere with the religion of both the Hindus and the Mahomedans. An accident set the whole country ablaze with mutiny. In 1857 a new rifle was issued to the troops and the cartridges for this rifle were covered with greased paper. The soldiers would have to bite these cartridges before they put them into their rifles and a story was spread about that the grease was made of a mixture of the fat of pigs and cows. To touch such a mixture would be defiling both the Hindus and the Mahomedans alike. Of course the story was quite untrue, but the sepoys were foolish enough to believe it. Many of them refused to touch the cartridges at all.

At Meerut, an important station near Delhi, the real Mutiny began. Some men of the 3rd Cavalry who had refused to use the cartridges were tried and imprisoned for their disobedience. On May 10th, the regiment broke into mutiny and released the prisoners and then the whole of the Indian troops in Meerut murdered their officers and set fire to the Cantonment. After this, they set off for Delhi, where they persuaded the troops there to mutiny also. They then proclaimed the old

Emperor Bahadur Shah II. as Emperor of India. Many of the English officers were murdered, but some managed to escape including one brave officer, Lieutenant Willoughby, who was in charge of the great magazine. He defended it bravely with a few men and then blew up the whole of it, to prevent its falling into the mutineers' hands. The mutiny spread rapidly over the provinces of Agra and Oudh and the Central Provinces as well. The Punjab alone remained loyal. The Bengal regiments in the province were disarmed by the prompt action of John Lawrence and the brave men who served under him — Neville Chamberlain, Herbert Edwardes and John Nicholson. In place of the mutinous regiments, new regiments of Sikhs and Punjabis were formed, who did their duty loyally in putting down the rebellion.

We have no space to tell the whole story of the great Mutiny but we will tell the story of the three cities chiefly connected with it — Cawnpore, Lucknow and Delhi.

At Cawnpore the rebels were led by Nana Sahib and his General Tantia Topee. Nana Sahib was the adopted son of the last Peshwa and he was angry with the English Government for refusing to give him the pension which his father had received.

The English in Cawnpore had unwisely taken refuge in a weak position outside the city and here the Nana besieged them. It was impossible to defend themselves in such a place, and finally the English General, Sir Hugh Wheeler, agreed to surrender if all the English were allowed to go down the river to Allahabad. To this Nana Sahib pretended to agree, but, when they were on board some boats in the river, he treacherously opened fire upon them. Nearly all the men were killed and the survivors, mostly women and children, were taken back to Cawnpore.

In the meantime help was coming. Colonel Henry Havelock, of whom we heard in the Persian War, was hurrying up from Calcutta with a small English force. In spite of the terrific heat his little army pressed on, defeated the rebels in several battles and finally arrived at Cawnpore in July. But he was too late to save the prisoners. They had all been murdered by the Nana's orders on the day before and their bodies thrown into a well. It is little wonder that Havelock's army made up their minds, after this terrible act of cruelty, that they would show no mercy to the mutineers.

We must now turn to the second great city—Lucknow. The troops there had mutinied and Sir Henry Lawrence, with a small body of English troops, a few faithful natives, and a large number of women and children, was besieged by them in the Residency. Sir Henry Lawrence was soon killed by a shell, but Colonel Inglis took his place and the siege went on. Day after day the gallant little garrison beat off the mutineers, till at last, in September 1857, Generals Outram and Havelock fought their way into Lucknow. But they were not strong to fight their way out again and so the siege went on. Finally, at the end of November, the brave defenders were relieved by an army under the new Commander-in-Chief, Sir Collin Campbell. Sir Henry Havelock, who had fought so gallantly, died just after the relief, worn out by his labours and hardships.

We must now turn to the great city of Delhi which was the real centre of the Mutiny, for within it was the ruler whom the mutineers had proclaimed Emperor of India. To end the Mutiny, Delhi must be taken. As soon as it could be collected, a small army occupied the Ridge—a low hill outside the city. This little force could not attack the rebels, but it maintained its position on the Ridge and waited for guns and reinforcements. General Anson, the Commander-in-Chief, died and General Barnard took his place. But in the meantime the new Commander-in-Chief, Sir Collin Campbell, an old and tried soldier, was on his way out from England. Gradually the little force in front of Delhi increased. Regiment after regiment came from the Punjab and siege guns began to arrive. General John Nicholson, the hero of Delhi, came down to take part in the siege and finally, in September, the attack began. The Kashmir Gate was blown up and the English entered the city. But there was several days' hard fighting in the streets. John Nicholson was mortally wounded, while gallantly leading his men. At last the English held the whole city. The Emperor fled but was pursued and captured. His sons, who were known to have been concerned in the murder of many Englishmen, were also captured and shot by Major Hodson.

The capture of Delhi was the beginning of the end. The mutineers were deprived of their headquarters and their leader. It only remained to subdue them. After the relief of Lucknow, Sir Collin Campbell had removed the sorely tried garrison and the city was in the hands of the mutineers. At the beginning of 1858 he advanced against it with a great army. In March the city was taken. In the meantime Sir Hugh Rose had led an army into Central India. Tantia Topi, the best leader that the mutineers produced, was crushed by him at Kalpi, and Jhansi, the centre of the Mutiny in that part of India, was taken in April 1858.

The real Mutiny was over, but it took some months before the different bands of mutineers were hunted down and broken up. It was not until July 1859 that Lord Canning was able to announce that peace once more reigned in India. But in the

Photo. Valentine, Dundee.

QUEEN VICTORIA.

STATUE AT THE IMPERIAL INSTITUTE, LONDON.

meantime a great change had taken place. The mistakes which led to the Mutiny had convinced the Imperial Government in England that it was time to make an end of the rule of the East India Company and to bring India under the direct rule of the Crown. And so, in August 1858, an Act passed through Parliament which did away with the old system. India was now to be governed by the Crown, through a new official, the Secretary of State for India. The Crown itself was to be represented in India by the Governor-General or Viceroy as he was now to be called.

On November 1st, 1858, this great change was publicly announced in India. Lord Canning the last Governor-General became the first Viceroy and so the old prophecy was made true. The old Raj of the Company had come to an end after hundred years. But India gained by being brought under the direct control of the English Sovereign.

"We declare it to be our royal will and pleasure that none be in anywise favoured, none molested or disquieted by reason of their religion, faith or observances: but that all shall alike enjoy the equal and impartial protection of the law."

In these and other gracious words Queen Victoria made known to her new subjects her intention towards them.

CHAPTER XXXIV.

THE FIRST VICEROYS.

LORD CANNING.

1858—1862.

Discontinuance of the system of 'lapse'—Military reforms—The Income-tax.

The first Viceroy had much work before him. Now that the great Mutiny was over, the system of government needed reforming and the whole army had to be remodelled. There was also the question of the punishment of those who had taken part in the Mutiny. Many people, enraged by some of the terrible deeds of the mutineers, demanded extreme punishment. But Lord Canning was wise enough to see that the time had come to be merciful. Those who were proved to have taken a leading part in the Mutiny were indeed punished. Tantia Topi was hanged. Nana Sahib disappeared and was never heard of again. The old Emperor, Bahadur Shah II., was put on his trial, found guilty, and sent to Burma where he died. But the mass of the people were allowed to go quietly back to their homes. During the Mutiny most of the ruling chiefs of India had loyally supported the government and helped to put down the mutineers. So it was determined, as a reward for this, to give up the system of 'lapse' which had been so freely used by Lord Dalhousie and to allow the rulers the right of adoption in future. Queen Victoria was pleased at this time to found a new order—the Star of India—and this was conferred as a mark of honour on all those rulers who had distinguished themselves by their loyalty.

It was now necessary to settle the condition of the army. The regiments which had taken part in the Mutiny mainly belonged to the army of Bengal. Most of these regiments disappeared altogether and those that remained were so remodelled that they contained soldiers of different classes. The new regiments of Sikhs, Punjabis and Pathans, which had been raised in the Punjab and had done such good service, were also taken into the army. The number of English officers with each regiment was reduced, but in future they were to do duty with their own regiments and not to go off on special appointments. Finally to guard against future danger, the number of English troops in the country was much increased and all the artillery, except a few mountain guns, remained in the hands of English gunners. A great deal of money had been spent in crushing the Mutiny and it was necessary to introduce some new taxation to pay for this. Therefore a new tax, the income-tax, was brought in.

By these, and other wise measures of reform, the country soon recovered its prosperity and the horrors of the Mutiny were soon forgotten.

Lord Canning remained in India till 1862, busily engaged in all these schemes of reform. Like Lord Dalhousie, he gave his life in the service of India. The labours and anxieties of his term of office had worn him out. Soon after his return to England he died.

LORD ELGIN.

1862—1863.

Lord Elgin, the new Viceroy, who had held several other important posts, had just returned from China, where he had successfully concluded the treaty which ended the Second Chinese War. He was an able man and began his term of office with a tour through the North of India. But he never returned from this. He was taken ill in the hills and died at Dharmsala in November 1863.

SIR JOHN (LORD) LAWRENCE.

1864—1869.

Bhutan War—Civil War in Afghanistan—Famine in Orissa—Relief works and preventive measures.

The Imperial Government now made up their minds to send out as Viceroy a man who knew India thoroughly and who was accustomed to the climate and so, in 1864, Sir John Lawrence, who had done so well in the Punjab during the Mutiny, was appointed Viceroy.

During his term of office trouble arose with Bhutan, a wild mountainous state, on the borders of Bengal. The English Government sent an ambassador to try and make some peaceful arrangement with the ruler of Bhutan but he was so badly treated that an army had to be sent. After a very little fighting, Bhutan gave way and agreed to hand over the passes leading into Bengal to the English. The safety of North Eastern Bengal was thus assured and the state of Bhutan has since remained friendly with the English government.

While Sir John Lawrence was Viceroy a civil war broke out in Afghanistan. The old Amir Dost Mahomed had died in 1863, and his sons were fighting for the throne. One of them, Sher Ali, appealed to the English for help. This was refused as the English government did not want to interfere in Afghanistan. In the end Sher Ali overcame his brothers, and became Amir. But he never forgave the English for not helping him and his hatred of them had important results some years later.

A terrible famine visited the province of Orissa in 1866. India has always been subject to such famines all through her history, but this was one of the worst that had ever occurred. Thousands of people perished. To put a stop to the famine, the government had to send large quantities of food into the province to be distributed among the starving people. To enable them to earn some money the government also started "relief works", that is the making of canals, etc., which would employ a large number of people. Since that time the government has always used such methods to relieve the sufferings of the people, whenever a famine breaks out.

Sir John Lawrence gave up his office in 1869. On his return to England he was made a peer, and became Lord Lawrence. For the rest of his life this great man and great Englishman busied himself in public affairs in England. He took a great interest in all public questions—particularly education. He died in 1879.

CHAPTER XXXV.

LORD MAYO.

1869 — 1872.

Decentralization of the Finances — Internal reforms — Relations with Frontier States.

The new Viceroy was the Earl of Mayo, an able man who soon became well liked in India. Soon after his arrival, he began to make some reforms in the government, particularly in the way in which money was spent. At this time the Council of the Viceroy consisted of seven members, one of whom was responsible for finance. Each year the amount of money which was spent came to more than the amount collected. This was not at all satisfactory and Lord Mayo made up his mind to find out the reason for it and to put a stop to it. He found out that the cause was that the governments of the different provinces were spending too much money. All the money received in revenue was paid by the different governments to the government of India and then each government sent in a statement of how much it wanted to spend in the year. As they could not always get all that they wanted, they made their statement as large as possible hoping to get more in this way. Lord Mayo stopped this and introduced a new system which is what we have to-day. By this system the government of each province receives a regular sum every year from the revenue. The government of the province can do as they please with this. They can either spend it all or, if they please, they may save some of it to spend on any scheme which they may have in hand for improving the province.

During his term of office Lord Mayo did his best to become friendly with the states on the borders of India. At that time there was a great deal of suspicion about the actions of Russia in Central Asia and the English government was anxious to be on friendly terms with the states on the borders of India, which lay between India and Russian Central Asia. So Lord Mayo held a durbar in 1869 at Ambala at which Sher Ali, the Amir was present. The Amir did not get all that he wanted, which was a regular treaty. Instead, however, Lord Mayo promised the friendship of the English government and told the Amir that, if necessary, he would give him arms and money. Lord Mayo also started friendly relations with the chiefs of Baluchistan who were afraid of an invasion from Persia, and English officers were sent to settle the boundary between Persia and Baluchistan.

Lord Mayo's term of office was a short one and ended in a very sad way. In 1872 he paid a visit to the Andaman Islands in the Bay of Bengal, to inspect the penal settlement there. While he was there he met his death, on February 8th, at the hand of one of the convicts.

LORD NORTHBROOK.

1872-1876.

Famine of 1874—Baroda affairs—Visit of the Prince of Wales (afterwards King Edward VII) to India.

The new Viceroy was Lord Northbrook. The first part of his term of office was quiet and peaceful but, in 1874, there was another outbreak of that curse of India—a famine. This time the famine was in Bengal. Thousands of people found themselves without food and the Government had to spend vast sums of money in providing for them.

During the same year the Viceroy had to interfere in the affairs of an Indian state—that of Baroda. Although, as we have seen, the native states had got back the right of adoption, yet this did not mean that they were free from control. The earlier Viceroys had made it quite clear that a native ruler was expected to govern his state fairly and justly and that, if he failed to do so, the English Government would interfere. It had been necessary to do so, in several smaller states, and now, in 1874, complaints were made about the way in which the Gaekwar of Baroda was governing. The government had warned him several times but he took no notice. And so an enquiry was held into his conduct before a committee of three English officials and three Indian princes. In the end, as it was proved that he had not governed at all properly, his state was taken away from him and given to a relation. Thus the government showed that they were ready to punish injustice even if the offender was in so high a position as the ruler of a state.

In 1875 the heir to the British throne—afterwards King Edward VII., Emperor of India—paid a visit to India. All classes of people in the country showed their loyalty and devotion and the great chiefs of India met their future ruler in a great durbar at Calcutta. The Prince of Wales afterwards made a grand tour in the North of India.

In 1876 Lord Northbrook resigned. A new Government had come into power in England which desired to send an ambassador to Kabul, although the Amir was unwilling to receive him. Lord Northbrook could not agree to this. He wished to leave things as they had been in the time of Lord Mayo and when the Government in England insisted, he sent in his resignation.

LORD LYTTON.

1876-1880.

Queen Victoria proclaimed Empress of India at the Durbar of 1877—Great famine of 1877—Second Afghan War—Treaty of Gandamak—Third Afghan War.

The Government now sent out Lord Lytton as Viceroy. Soon after his arrival Queen Victoria was pleased to take the title of Empress of India.

A splendid durbar was held at Delhi on January 1st. 1877, for the purpose of proclaiming the new title and, at the same time, Queen Victoria was pleased to announce the foundation of a new order—that of the Indian Empire.

The rejoicing of India was somewhat checked by another terrible famine which visited Southern India in the same year.

Lord Lytton had been sent by the Government to carry out what was called a "forward policy" in Afghanistan and along the frontier. The Government in England were very suspicious of Russia and they believed that the Amir was plotting with Russia against England. For this reason they wished to keep an English ambassador in Kabul. But the Amir was unwilling to agree to this and instead, in 1876, sent an ambassador to Simla to try and come to some understanding with the Viceroy.

But nothing resulted from the visit and in the meantime the English strengthened their hold upon the frontier by occupying Quetta in Baluchistan, by an arrangement with the Khan of Khelat. In 1877 there was another meeting between an Afghan ambassador and Sir L. Pelly, who represented the Viceroy, at Peshawar. But the English still insisted on a British ambassador living in Afghanistan and the Amir still refused.

In the meantime England and Russia were very nearly at war in Europe. England had begun to prepare for war and brought troops from India to Malta. In reply to this the Russians sent an ambassador to Kabul to try and make a treaty with the Amir (1878). When the Viceroy learnt of this, he informed the Amir that he insisted on sending an English ambassador also to Kabul. The Amir refused to let him enter the country and so the Second Afghan War began. At the end of 1878 three Armies under Generals Browne, Stewart, and Roberts (afterwards Lord Roberts) entered the country. Several fortresses were captured and the Amir fled northwards where he died (February 1879). His son Yakub Khan then came to an arrangement with the English by the Treaty of Gandamak, May 1879. By this treaty the English were to keep a resident in Afghanistan and to control the foreign relations of the country—that is, the Afghans were not to deal with any other country except through the English Government.

The English resident was Major Sir Louis Cavagnari and he arrived in Kabul in July 1879. He was well received and at first all went well. But in September a riot broke out in Kabul and the resident and his staff were all murdered. Yakub Khan now insisted on abdicating and gave himself up to the English who sent him to India where he spent the rest of his life. In the meantime General Roberts had advanced and taken Kabul where he maintained order. General Stewart remained at Kandahar till March 1880 when he left a small garrison behind him and marched with his main army to Kabul to General Roberts. On the way he fought and won the battle of Ahmed Khel. While all this was happening a new Government had come into power in England. The new Government regarded the whole "forward policy" in Afghanistan as a great mistake and Lord Ripon was sent out in place of Lord Lytton, with orders to stop the war as soon as possible.

CHAPTER XXXVI.

LORD RIPON.

1880—1884.

The march to Kandahar—Abdul Rahman proclaimed Amir of Afghanistan—Local Self-Government Act.

The new Viceroy was not a stranger to Indian affairs, for he had been Secretary of State for India in a former Government in England. He was full of ideas of reform, but he had first to bring the Afghan War to an end.

In the meantime that war still went on. A large Afghan force under Ayub Khan, the brother of the late Amir, advanced upon Kandahar. General Primrose, who commanded the English garrison in that city, sent out a small army under General Burrowes against the Afghans.

The force was much too small and was badly defeated by Ayub Khan at Maiwand (July 27th 1880). The garrison of Kandahar was now cut off. General Stewart, who commanded at Kabul, now sent General Roberts, with 10,000 men, to relieve Kandahar. The famous march to Kandahar took twenty-two days—from August 9th to August 31st 1880. Hurrying along as fast as he could,

Lord Roberts reached Kandahar on August 31st and defeated the Afghans outside the city. Kandahar was saved and for this great service, General Roberts was made Lord Roberts of Kandahar. This great soldier lived to do splendid service in other parts of the Empire also. He died in 1914 while on a visit to the army serving in Belgium. There were few generals more beloved by their troops, both English and Indian alike.

In the meantime a new Amir had been found for Afghanistan, in the person of Abdur Rahman, a grandson of Dost Mahomed. He was proclaimed Amir in July 1880 and then the English gradually withdrew their armies from the country. Since that time relations between the two countries have been friendly.

Lord Ripon's term of office is chiefly remembered for the Self-Government Act (1882), which introduced into India the methods of local government which are to be found in England. By this act municipal boards or committees were set up, most of the members of which were elected by the people.

The Boards had the work of keeping towns and villages clean and healthy, lighting and repairing the roads, maintaining a supply of good water and many other useful duties, entrusted to them.

Larger Boards called District Boards were also set up which could control the work of the municipal boards in the district under them. Both boards were given power to raise taxes on land, houses, etc., for the purpose of providing money for the work which they had to do.

Lord Ripon resigned in 1884.

LORD DUFFERIN.

1884—1888.

The Panjdeh incident—Third Burmese War—Annexation of Upper Burma—Gwalior restored to Sindia—The Indian National Congress.

The Earl of Dufferin, the next Viceroy, was a statesman of much experience. He had been Governor-General of Canada and had been Ambassador to several European countries.

Very soon after his arrival, a dispute arose, known as the Panjdeh incident, which nearly led to trouble with Russia. Some Turkomans, who were under the protection of Russia, claimed some territory on the borders of Afghanistan and, in 1885, they advanced, with a small force of Russians to help them, to take possession of the territory. The Amir sent troops to oppose them and it seemed as if there would be war. England could not see Afghanistan, a friendly state upon her frontier, attacked without interfering, and made a protest to the Russian Government. Fortunately good sense prevented war and an arrangement was made which satisfied both parties.

In 1885, the last Burmese War broke out. Ever since the earlier wars the King of Burma had behaved extremely badly to the English companies in the country and was also a very cruel ruler to his own people. As he took no notice of the warnings that were sent to him, war was declared. Mandalay was captured. King Thebaw was taken prisoner and exiled to India and, in 1886, the whole of Upper Burma became an English possession. This was the last great addition to the territories of the Indian Empire.

Lord Dufferin continued the policy begun by Lord Ripon of giving back their 'powers' to those Indian rulers who showed themselves fit to govern their own territories. In this way Mysore (1881) and Gwalior (1885) were both given back to their own chiefs.

In Lord Dufferin's time National Congresses began to be held. The Self-Government Act had given the people of India an interest in the government of the country and they now showed this by holding great meetings of representatives from all over the country to talk over matters of general interest.

Lord Dufferin retired in 1888 and was promoted on his departure from India with the title of "Marquis of Dufferin and Ava."

LORD LANSDOWNE.

1888—1894.

Rising in Manipur—Reconstruction of the Legislative Councils.

The new Viceroy was the Marquis of Lansdowne, and his term of office was quiet and peaceful. A rebellion which broke out in the small state of Manipur, to the south of Assam, in which the British Commissioner of Assam was murdered (1891), was soon put down. The frontier was strengthened during this period and the small state of Sikkim, in which is situated Darjeeling, the summer capital of Bengal, was taken under the protection of the English by an arrangement with the Chinese Government (1890).

The principle of elected members was extended (1892) to both the Provincial Legislative Councils and also to that of the Supreme Government. Both Councils were increased in size and the new members were to be elected. Lord Lansdowne retired in 1894.

LORD ELGIN.

1894—1898

Delimitation of Frontier boundaries — Chitral expedition — Army reorganization — The Plague.

The Earl of Elgin was the son of the former Viceroy who had died in India (1863).

During his time the strengthening of the frontier went on. The wild tribes who lived on the border were kept in order and when they rebelled, as they did at Chitral in 1895, a strong force was sent against them.

The Army of India was reorganised at this time. There had been originally three armies—those of Bengal, Madras and Bombay—each with its own organization. But this was now done away with and the whole army was put under one Commander-in-Chief.

During Lord Elgin's time, that terrible scourge, the plague, appeared in India. It is said to have come from China and the great port of Bombay was the scene of many hundreds of deaths. The Government had to take strong measures to prevent the disease from spreading. But many of the people from ignorance resisted the work of the doctors and some rioting took place. Since that time, the plague has unfortunately become a regular disease in

India. But the doctors now know the proper treatment for the disease and the people are now wise enough to help them and assist in putting down the disease. Lord Elgin retired in 1894.

CHAPTER XXXVII.

THE LATER VICEROYS.

LORD CURZON.

1899 — 1905.

Famine of 1900 — Frontier policy — Creation of a new province: the United Provinces — Planning of the great canal system of the Punjab — The Durbar of 1903 — Visit of the Prince and Princess of Wales — Partition of Bengal — Expedition to Thibet.

The new Viceroy was Lord Curzon, a hard working and able man who introduced a number of reforms. A terrible famine broke out in 1900 in the Centre and South of India and the government had to spend very large sums of money in relieving the miseries of the starving people.

Lord Curzon did much to strengthen the frontier, particularly on the North-West. As we have seen the tribes on the border were wild and lawless and needed much watching. Lord Curzon brought in a new scheme. He started a force for the frontier formed from the border tribes themselves, and called the frontier militia. It was the business of this militia — which was placed under English officers — to maintain order. At the same time, Lord Curzon took away the districts of the North-West Frontier from the province of the Punjab and made them into a new province — the North-West Frontier Province. The old North-West Provinces of Agra and Oudh were given a new name — the United Provinces.

Lord Curzon's other reforms were many. He appointed a committee to enquire into the canal system and to try and improve it, for, where there is water, there is less danger of famine, and one of the results of this was the planning of the great canal system of the Punjab which is still being completed. In this way hundreds of miles of desert land will in time become rich and fertile. Education was improved under Lord Curzon and Chiefs Colleges were established for the education of the sons of the princes and chiefs of India.

In the year 1901 the great and wise Queen Empress, who had taken India under her protection, passed away, after a long and splendid reign of sixty-three years. Her son Edward VII. — whom we saw visiting India in 1875 — succeeded her as King Emperor. At a splendid durbar held in Delhi in 1903 the new King Emperor was proclaimed as Emperor of India.

During Lord Curzon's time The Prince and Princess of Wales — our present King Emperor and Empress — visited India and were received with great expressions of rejoicing and loyalty.

Lord Curzon's last two great acts were the partition of Bengal and the expedition to Thibet. Bengal had become a very large province and it seemed to be a better arrangement to divide it up. And so, in 1904, the eastern part, with Assam, was made into a separate province called Eastern Bengal.

The expedition to Thibet was the result of the Dalai Llama — the ruler of that country — refusing to keep a treaty which he had made with the English Government to allow traders to visit his country. After some fighting (1904), Lhassa, the capital, was reached. A peace was made by which the Thibetans agreed to open up their country to traders from India.

In 1905, Lord Curzon, who had some difference of opinion with the Government in England about the reform of the army, and the position of the Commander-in-Chief, resigned his office and returned to England.

LORD MINTO.

1905 — 1910.

The India Council Act.

The new Viceroy, the Earl of Minto, had an able Secretary of State, Lord Morley, to help him and they produced, in 1909, the Indian Council Act.

This act carried on the earlier work begun by Lord Ripon. By it the Legislative Councils of the different provinces have a much larger number of elected members than before. This gives the people of the country a still greater interest in its affairs. Over all these councils is the Imperial Council of the Viceroy. On this Council are representatives of the different provinces, and all the great interests of the country—trade, law, etc.,—are represented upon it. By this act every citizen of the country is made to feel that he is able to help in the progress and welfare of India. It is yet too early for us to see the great results which may come from this reform.

Lord Minto retired in 1910. In his last year the great and good King Emperor Edward VII.—who was called the Peacemaker, from his desire to be on peaceful terms with all nations—died after a short reign (May 6th, 1910) and was succeeded by his son, our present King Emperor, George V.

Photo. Bourne and Shepherd, India.

THE DELHI DURBAR OF 1903.

LORD HARDINGE.

1910.

The great Coronation Durbar of 1911 — Delhi made the capital of India — Partition of Bengal annulled.

Our present Viceroy arrived in November 1910. We will close our History by a few words about that great event which took place in the following year — the great Coronation Durbar of 1911.

In 1911, when it was announced that, after his Coronation in England, His Majesty would be graciously pleased to visit his Indian Empire, all India was filled with excitement and great preparations began. His Majesty and his father had both visited India as Prince of Wales, but the reigning sovereign had never done so before. In December 1911, the great Durbar took place at Delhi — the most splendid gathering that had ever been seen in India.

The King Emperor having announced his accession to the throne and his Coronation, then announced his pleasure that

1. Delhi should once more become the capital of India.

2. Bengal should become one province again under a Governor.

His Majesty made other gracious announcements—the granting of the Victoria Cross (the highest decoration for bravery) to Indian soldiers being one of them. And so the great durbar came to an end.

And so we have come to the end of our long story. We have seen early India with its wild tribes, we have seen empires and kingdoms rise and fall and finally we see India to-day—an Empire itself and yet part of a greater Empire, the largest and freest that the world has ever seen.

CHAPTER XXXVIII.

Now that we have told the long story of the History of India from its earliest days down to the present time, we cannot do better than conclude it by a general summary of all that we have read.

To do this it is better to divide our story into three main divisions—the Hindu, the Mahomedan, and the British periods.

The first of these begins with the very earliest days, the second may begin with the invasion of Mahmud of Ghazni in A. D. 1000 and the third from the Battle of Plassey (1757). Of course this division is only a rough one.

We know that there were Mahomedans in India before Mahmud's invasion, and we know that the English came to India long before 1757. But for a general summary these are very convenient dates to take.

THE HINDU PERIOD.

As we have seen in our earlier chapters, we know very little about the first part of this period. From the Vedas we learn of the early invasions of

India by the Aryans, and we know something of the habits of these early peoples. We also know that there were other peoples in India before the Aryans came, for when the system of 'caste' was introduced, the lowest caste, the Sudras, was composed of the descendants of these people and also of those of mixed blood. And then gradually the different tribes and families of Aryan invaders became organized into kingdoms and states, which were strong enough to raise large armies like that which opposed Alexander the Great in 327 B. C.

Soon we came to the foundation of the great Mauryan Empire, the first real empire in India, which lasted for so long and which produced great kings like Chandragupta and Asoka. During this time the Buddhist religion was the chief force in the country, and we know from the writings of the Chinese travellers how the country was full of Buddhist monasteries and Buddhist monuments, many of which we can still see to-day.

The Mauryan Empire passes away and northern invaders enter India, bringing with them some of the Greek influence left behind by the Empire of Alexander and the kingdoms formed after his death. Then, after a period of confusion, follows another great Empire — the Gupta. During the existence of this Empire the religion of Brahmanism gradually overcomes the Buddhist religion and the latter, as we have seen, disappears from India.

The Gupta Empire gradually becomes weaker and weaker, and breaks up into a number of small pieces towards the end of the fifth century A. D. At this time a new force arises in India—the brave warlike Rajput clans, each with its own leader. They were brave enough soldiers but they could not unite among themselves. This made India weak and open to invasion. When a rich country is too weak or too disunited to protect itself, it will soon become the prey of stronger and better organized forces from outside. Down from the north came the Mahomedans. India was too weak to resist them, and the Hindu period of its History comes to an end.

THE MAHOMEDAN PERIOD.

We have already considered the formation of Islam, and we have seen how the new religion united its followers together into large and powerful armies. These armies were inspired by two main ideas—the conquest of the non-Mahomedan peoples and the spread of their own religion. We may begin our account of the Mahomedan period with the year 1000 A. D., although smaller bands of Mahomedan invaders had appeared in India before that date. In that year came the first great invasion, that of Mahmud of Ghazni whom men called the 'Image Breaker.' Again and again he invaded India, plundering, burning and destroying temples. Soon after him comes Mahomed Ghori who also plundered and destroyed. But he left behind him something more permanent than Mahmud of Ghazni had done. He set up one of his generals as ruler of Delhi in 1206. This ruler was the first of a dynasty called the Slave kings. From that time down to 1857 there was always a Mahomedan ruler in Delhi. The Slave kings passed away and were succeeded by family after family of kings, some strong, some weak. But still India was divided and disunited, so that when new invaders came in the sixteenth century, they were successful in conquering the country. The new conquerors were called 'Moguls,' but were really Turks. They were a strong vigorous people, reared in a cold bracing climate. In 1526 Babar—who was a descendant of the great conqueror Timur—overthrew the Mahomedan kingdom of Delhi, defeated the Rajputs and founded what we call the Mogul Empire. The great days of this Empire last till the death of Aurungzeb in 1707. Babar and his successors—the greatest of whom was Akbar—were capable rulers and organizers. They built up a great system of government, some remains of which have lasted down to our own days. Although Mahomedans by religion, they were tolerant of other beliefs, and so we find Hindus entering their service and holding offices under them. The great Akbar married a Rajput princess, and was distinguished for the great interest that he took in all religions, including Christianity, for by this time Christian missionaries had begun to visit India. But the last great Mogul, Aurungzeb, was not so wise. A very zealous Mahomedan, he persecuted other religions and so raised up enemies on every side. The most powerful of these were the Marathas. The last thirty years of his reign were spent in ceaseless fighting, and when he died, in 1707, he had so weakened his Empire that the Marathas seemed the future rulers of the country. But down from the north came Nadir Shah and his hardy Persian hosts, and the battle of Panipat (1761) broke the Maratha power. The Mogul Empire never recovered from the shock and though there was still a nominal emperor at Delhi, his power soon became a mere shadow and a new power arose in the country.

THE BRITISH PERIOD.

We have seen in our earlier chapters how the different European powers arrived in India — Portugese, Dutch, French, English—and how they obtained trading stations at different ports. We have read of the decay of the Portugese power, and of the great Frenchman Dupleix and his dream of a French Empire in India, which was overthrown by the genius of Clive. It is with Clive's great victory of Plassey (1757) that we may begin the British period. From that time the East India Company gradually finds itself transformed from a simple trading company into a ruling power. First Bengal comes under its administration. Then come the wars with Haidar Ali and his son Tipu, which end in the fall of the Mysore kingdom and the supremacy of the Company in the South (1799). The Company itself has had to be remodelled to suit its new position as a ruler, and the Act of 1784 brings the Governor-Generals directly in contact with the Home Government. Then follows the period of the early Maratha wars and of the 'subsidiary treaties.' The Emperor still reigns at Delhi, but he is a mere shadow, and he reigns at the pleasure of new masters. Further disturbances lead to the extinction of the Maratha power, and the rule of the Company is extended to portions of Burma and even to distant Singapore. In 1845 the First Sikh War breaks out. We have studied the history of the Sikhs in an earlier chapter, and need not here repeat it in detail. The firm hand of Ranjit Singh had built up a strong kingdom out of the disorderly Sikh confederacies, but on his death (1839) a period of confusion follows, which ends in a Sikh invasion of the territory under the protection of the Company. The First Sikh War ends in victory for the English, but it is only a brief pause. Further disorders convince the great Governor-General, Dalhousie, that annexation is the only remedy, and the Second Sikh War (1848) results in the final extinction of the Sikh power and the addition of the Punjab to the Company's territories. Oudh, too, is annexed.

Nine years pass away and the discontent in the country -- more particularly among the troops — comes to a head in the Indian Mutiny of 1857. Its results are far reaching. The day of the old Company is done. Convinced that direct Imperial control is the only satisfactory method of government for the country, the Queen assumes the 'government of the territories in India, hitherto administered in trust for us by the Honourable East India Company' (1858). Nineteen years later (1877) the assumption of the Imperial title, Empress of India, makes the position of the sovereign still clearer to her Indian subjects. The various royal visits to India, culminating in the memorable Durbar of 1911, have still further intensified the connection.

We need not pursue the History of the country under Imperial control. Despite the effects of famine, plague, and the other evils to which India is subject, the History of the last fifty years has been one of material prosperity and progress. To attempt to give an account of such progress and expansion in detail would require a separate volume. The territories of the Empire — with the exception of Upper Burma annexed in 1886, after the Second Burmese War — have not been expanded to any great extent. Rather, as we have said above, expansion has taken place in the material prosperity of the population. One has only to consider the vast network of railways, the huge system of canals, the ever expanding seaports, and the system of public instruction extending its schools and colleges to every quarter of the peninsula, to realize the great work that has been done.

CHRONOLOGICAL TABLE OF INDIAN HISTORY.

HINDU PERIOD.

B.C.

600 (about). Brahmanism or Hinduism—the chief religion of India.

567. Birth of Gautama (the Buddha).

550 (about). Establishment of the Kingdom of Magadha.

500 (about). Invasion of the Punjab by the Persians.

327. Invasion of India by Alexander the Great.

326. Victory over Porus on the Jhelum.

320. Establishment of the Maurya Empire by Chandragupta.

299 (about). Accession of Bindusara.

272 (about). Accession of Asoka.

232 (about). Death of Asoka.

180 (about). Break-up of the Maurya Empire. Rise of the Andhra kings.

160 (about). Invasion of the Sakas and Pallavas.

A.D.

120 (about). Accession of Kanishka. (Kushan dynasty.)

150. Death of Kanishka.

320 (about). Rise of the Gupta Empire under Chandragupta.

326. Accession of Samudragupta.

375. Accession of Chandragupta Vikramaditya.

413. Death of Chandragupta Vikramaditya.

480. Fall of the Gupta Empire.

608. Establishment of the Kingdom of Kanauj by King Harsha.
Rise of the Deccan Kingdom under Pulikesin II. (Chalukya dynasty).
642. Death of Pulikesin II.
648. Death of Harsha. Break-up of the Kingdom of Kanauj.
700-1000. Gradual ascendency of the Rajputs.

MAHOMEDAN PERIOD.

A. D.
570. Birth of Mahomed at Mecca.
632. Death of Mahomed.
712. First Mahomedan invasion of India under Mahomed bin Kasim.
1000. Invasion of India by Mahmud of Ghazni; defeat of Raja Jaipal of Lahore.
1018. Destruction of Kanauj by Mahmud of Ghazni.
1026. Capture of Somnath by Mahmud of Ghazni.
1030. Death of Mahmud of Ghazni.
1174. Accession of Mahomed Ghori.
1191. Invasion of India by Mahomed Ghori. Victory of Prithvi Raj at Tarain.
1192. Second Invasion of India by Mahomed Ghori. Prithvi Raj defeated and captured at Tarain.
1206. Death of Mahomed Ghori. Kutb-ud-din establishes the Slave dynasty at Delhi.
1210. Death of Kutb-ud-din.
1211. Accession of Altamsh.
1236. Death of Altamsh.
1266. Accession of Balban.
1287. Death of Balban. Establishment of the Khilji dynasty.

1296. Accession of Ala-ud-din.
1297. Invasion of the Tartars. Victory of Ala-ud-din over the Tartars near Delhi.
1303. Siege and capture of Chitor by Ala-ud-din.
1316. Death of Ala-ud-din. Accession of Kutb-ud-din Mubarak.
1320. Establishment of the Tughlak dynasty by Ghias-ud-din Tughlak.
1325. Death of Ghias-ud-din. Accession of Mahomed Tughlak.
1351. Death of Mahomed Tughlak. Accession of Firoz Shah.
1388. Death of Firoz Shah.
1398. Invasion of Timur.
1412. Death of Mahomed, the last of the Tughlak dynasty.
1478. Establishment of the Lodi dynasty.
1526. Invasion of India by Babar. Death of the last Lodi king at the battle of Panipat. Establishment of the Mogul Empire.
1527. Overthrow of the Rajputs by Babar at Kanwaha.
1530. Death of Babar. Accession of Humayun.
1539. Defeat of Humayun by Sher Khan.
1540. Defeat of Humayun by Sher Khan at Kanauj. Flight of Humayun.
1545. Death of Sher Khan (Sher Shah).
1555. Return of Humayun to Delhi.
1556. Death of Humayun. Accession of Akbar.
Akbar's victory of Panipat reestablishes Mogul Empire: (Second battle of Panipat.)
1567. Capture of Chitor by Akbar.
1605. Death of Akbar. Accession of Jehangir.
1626. Rebellion of Mahabat Khan.
1627. Death of Jehangir. Accession of Shah Jehan.
1636. Conquest of part of the Deccan.
1648. The Taj Mahal completed.

1658. Shah Jehan imprisoned by Aurungzeb. Accession of Aurungzeb.

1671. The Marathas under Sivaji plunder Surat and defeat the armies of Aurungzeb.

1680. Death of Sivaji.

1686. Capture of Bijapur.

1687. Capture of Golconda.

1689. Capture and death of Sambhaji, son of Sivaji.

1707. Death of Aurungzeb. Accession of Bahadur Shah.

1708. Death of Guru Gobind Singh, the last Guru who had made the Sikhs a fighting race.

1712. Death of Bahadur Shah. Accession of Jahandar Shah.

1713. Death of Jahandar. Accession of Farukhsiyar.

1719. Death of Farukhsiyar. Accession of Mahomed Shah.

1722. The Deccan becomes practically independent under Asif Jah.

1738. The Maratha Invasion of the Empire from the South. Invasion of the Persians under Nadir Shah. Battle of Karnal. Capture and sack of Delhi.

1748. Invasion of the Afghans under Ahmed Shah Durani. Victory of Mahomed Shah at Sirhind.

Death of Mahomed Shah. Accession of Ahmed Shah.

1752. Second invasion of the Afghans under Ahmed Shah Durani.

1754. The Emperor Ahmed Shah deposed. Accession of Alamgir II.

1756. Third Afghan invasion under Ahmed Shah Durani. Plunder of Delhi.

1759. Murder of Alamgir II. His successor, Shah Alum II, flees to Bengal. Fourth Afghan invasion under Ahmed Shah Durani.

1761. Third battle of Panipat, in which combined Mogul and Maratha armies are defeated by the Afghans under Ahmed Shah Durani.

BRITISH PERIOD.

[1498. Vasco da Gama's voyage to Calicut.]
[1510. Foundation of Goa by Albuquerque.]
1600. Foundation of the East India Company.
1612. The East India Company open their first trading port at Surat.
1615. Embassy of Sir Thomas Roe to the Court of Jehangir.
1639. Foundation of Fort St. George, Madras.
1640. Foundation of settlements on the Hughli.
1661. Acquisition of Bombay by the English from Portugal.
1664. Foundation of the French East India Company.
1667. Foundation of the first French settlement at Surat.
1674. Foundation of the French settlement at Pondicherry.
1686. Foundation of Calcutta — Fort William — by Job Charnock.
1742. Arrival of Dupleix as Governor of Pondicherry.
1743. England and France at war.
1746. Madras surrendered to the French. Battle of San Thomé.
1748. Peace between England and France.
1751. Capture and defence of Arcot by Clive.
1752. Defeat of the French and their allies at Srirangam.
1754. Recall of Dupleix to France.
1756. England and France at war.
1757. The Black Hole of Calcutta.
Victory of Clive at Plassey.
1760. Victory of Coote over the French at Wandiwash.
1761. Capture of Pondicherry by Coote.
1764. Battle of Buxar.
1767. Departure of Clive from India.
Outbreak of war between Haidar Ali of Mysore and the English.

1772. Arrival of Warren Hastings in Bengal.
1773. The Regulating Act passed.
1774. Warren Hastings, first Governor-General.
1780. Maratha War. Capture of Gwalior.
Second Mysore War begins.
1781. Battle of Porto Novo.
1782. Treaty of Salbai between the English and Marathas. Death of Haidar Ali.
1784. Treaty of Mangalore between the English and Tipu.
1785. Departure of Warren Hastings.
1786. Arrival of Lord Cornwallis as Governor-General.
1790. Third Mysore War begins.
1792. Peace between the English and Tipu.
1793. The Permanent Settlement of Bengal. Departure of Lord Cornwallis. Sir John Shore, Governor-General.
1798. Departure of Sir John Shore. Arrival of Lord Mornington (Marquis of Wellesley).
1799. Fourth Mysore War. Capture of Seringapatam. Death of Tipu.
1801. The English acquire the Carnatic.
1803. Second Maratha War. Battles of Assaye and Argaon. Capture of Delhi by Lake. The Emperor (Shah Alum II.) taken under English protection. Battle of Laswari.
1805. Departure of Lord Wellesley. Arrival of Lord Cornwallis. Death of Lord Cornwallis. Sir G. Barlow, Governor-General.
1807. Arrival of Lord Minto as Governor-General.
1809. Treaty of Amritsar between Ranjit Singh and the English.
1810. Capture of Mauritius from the French.
1811. Capture of Java from the Dutch (given back 1815).
1813. The East India Company's monopoly abolished. Departure of Lord Minto. Arrival of Lord Hastings.

1814-16. The Gurkha wars. Treaty of Sagauli between the Gurkhas and the English.

1817-18. The Pindari wars. Last Maratha War. Extinction of Maratha power.

1819. Conquest of Ceylon completed.
Foundation of Singapore by Sir S. Raffles.

1822. Departure of Lord Hastings.

1823. Arrival of Lord Amherst.

1824. First Burmese War begins.

1825. Capture of Prome.

1826. Treaty of Yandabu. The Burmese surrender Assam, Tennasserim and Arakan.

1828. Departure of Lord Amherst. Arrival of Lord William Bentinck.

1829. Abolition of Sati.

1835. Departure of Lord William Bentinck. Sir C. Metcalfe, Governor-General.

1836. Departure of Sir C. Metcalfe. Arrival of Lord Auckland.

1837. Embassy of Burnes to Kabul.

1838. Attack on Herat by the Persians. Outbreak of the First Afghan War.

1839. Kabul captured. Shah Shuja proclaimed Amir.
Death of Ranjit Singh.

1841. Outbreak in Kabul. Murder of Burnes and Macnaghten.

1842. The retreat from Kabul. Departure of Lord Auckland. Arrival of Lord Ellenborough.

1843. End of the First Afghan War. Battle of Miani and conquest of Sind.

1844. Recall of Lord Ellenborough. Arrival of Sir H. Hardinge.

1845. First Sikh War. Battles of Mudki and Ferozeshah.

1846. First Sikh War. Battles of Aliwal and Sobraon. Treaty of Lahore.

1848. Departure of Lord Hardinge. Arrival of Lord Dalhousie.
Outbreak of Second Sikh War.

1849. Second Sikh War. Battles of Chilianwalah and Gujrat. Annexation of the Punjab.

1852. Second Burmese War. Annexation of Lower Burma.

1856. Annexation of Oudh. Departure of Lord Dalhousie. Arrival of Lord Canning.

1857. Outbreak of the Indian Mutiny. Proclamation of Bahadur Shah II. as Emperor at Delhi. Massacre of Cawnpore. Defence of Lucknow. Capture of Delhi.

1858. Capture of Lucknow. Mutiny gradually suppressed in Central India. Abolition of the rule of the East India Company. Royal Proclamation. Lord Canning, first Viceroy.

1862. Departure of Lord Canning. Arrival of Lord Elgin.

1863. Death of Lord Elgin.

1864. Arrival of Sir J. (Lord) Lawrence.

1866. Outbreak of famine in Orissa. Relief works first started.

1869. Departure of Lord Lawrence. Arrival of Lord Mayo.

1872. Murder of Lord Mayo. Arrival of Lord Northbrook.

1874. Great famine in Bengal.

1875. Visit of H. R. H. the Prince of Wales (afterwards King Edward VII.) to India.

1876. Departure of Lord Northbrook. Arrival of Lord Lytton.

1877. Queen Victoria proclaimed Empress of India at Delhi.

1878. Outbreak of the Second Afghan War.

1879. Treaty of Gandamak. Arrival of Sir L. Cavagnari in Kabul. Outbreak in Kabul. Cavagnari murdered.

1880. Battle of Ahmed Khel. Lord Lytton resigns. Arrival of Lord Ripon. Battle of Maiwand. Robert's march to Kandahar. End of the war and withdrawal of the English.